KU-511-098

*SUNDAY TIMES* BESTSELLING AUTHOR

# CASEY WATSON

# Too Hurt to Stay

The true story of a troubled boy's
desperate search for a loving home

HARPER
element

This book is a work of non-fiction based on the author's experiences.
In order to protect privacy, names, identifying characteristics,
dialogue and details have been changed or reconstructed.

HarperElement
An imprint of HarperCollins*Publishers*
77–85 Fulham Palace Road,
Hammersmith, London W6 8JB

www.harpercollins.co.uk

and HarperElement are trademarks of
HarperCollins*Publishers* Ltd

First published by HarperElement 2012

1 3 5 7 9 10 8 6 4 2

© Casey Watson 2012

Casey Watson asserts the moral right to
be identified as the author of this work

A catalogue record of this book
is available from the British Library

ISBN 978-0-00-743662-0

Printed and bound in Great Britain by
Clays Ltd, St Ives plc

All rights reserved. No part of this publication may be
reproduced, stored in a retrieval system, or transmitted,
in any form or by any means, electronic, mechanical,
photocopying, recording or otherwise, without the prior
written permission of the publishers.

**MIX**
Paper from
responsible sources
**FSC** **FSC˚ C007454**
www.fsc.org

FSC™ is a non-profit international organisation established to promote
the responsible management of the world's forests. Products carrying the
FSC label are independently certified to assure consumers that they come
from forests that are managed to meet the social, economic and
ecological needs of present and future generations,
and other controlled sources.

Find out more about HarperCollins and the environment at
**www.harpercollins.co.uk/green**

*To my wonderful and supportive family*

# Acknowledgements

I would like to thank all of the team at HarperCollins, the lovely Andrew Lownie, and my friend and mentor, Lynne. I'd also like to add a special thought to all those working within the care system.

# Chapter 1

They always say a change is as good as a rest, don't they? And let's face it, who wants to put their feet up and do nothing all day long? Not me.

Which was just as well. It was mid-August, a time of year where rest tends to be high on the agenda, but as I hefted my number one grandson from his car seat, my principal thought was 'fat chance'.

I didn't like to admit it, because at forty-three I was young for a granny, but four hours in town with my daughter Riley and her two little ones had exhausted me. Not that I hadn't asked for it. I'd been itching to spend more time with Levi and Jackson, so I had no business moaning and groaning about it. And besides, I well remembered how tiring it was being a young mum with two little ones to run around after; with Levi almost three now and Jackson just six months old, Riley had her work cut out.

And I remembered how tiring childcare could be better than most grannies, maybe. We'd just said goodbye to our

1

last foster children, and though at ten and seven Ashton and Olivia hadn't exactly been toddlers, they had certainly been as challenging as little ones. As with all the kids we took, these had been profoundly damaged children, so caring for them had definitely taken its toll.

'God, I could kill for a coffee,' I told Riley as we got the kids indoors and settled them in the living room with some toys.

'You sit down,' she said. 'I'll deal with the drinks.' But almost as soon as I'd lowered myself and the baby into an armchair with a picture book, the phone rang. Levi shot to his feet.

Which meant I had to be quick. He was three now and his most favourite thing at the moment was to chat on the phone. Needless to say, he beat me to it.

'Hiya!' he was babbling into the receiver. 'Hiya! Lub you!' Then his usual follow-up. 'Okay, then. Byeee!'

I gently prised the receiver from him, despite his indignant protests, and hoped whoever was on the end hadn't already hung up. Happily he hadn't – it was John Fulshaw, our fostering-agency link worker – though he'd been about to. 'Thought I'd dialled a wrong number,' he chuckled. 'Either that or you were doing a bit of moonlighting. Thought you'd wanted a break!'

'It's Levi,' I told him. 'And this *is* my break. Anyway, to what do I owe the pleasure?'

'My, he's growing up fast,' John said. Then he cleared his throat. It was a sign I knew of old. A sign that invariably meant that the tone of the conversation was about to change.

'So?' I asked.

'So, talking of breaks,' he continued, 'we...ll, I just wondered how adamant you felt on that front?'

'Go on,' I said slowly, while pulling a face at Riley. She was standing in the kitchen doorway, listening.

'Well,' John said again, obviously limbering up still, 'we just wondered what the chances were of you taking on another placement. It's not going to be long term ...'

'Yeah, right. Heard that one before, John.'

'No, this time I'm sure of it. The plan here is for the child to be returned home to his family as soon as possible.'

Which seemed odd. My husband Mike and I didn't do mainstream fostering. We were specialist carers, trained to deliver a behaviour-modification programme that was geared to helping the most profoundly damaged kids. These were kids that were too challenging to be fostered in the mainstream, and for whom the alternative was often the grim option of a secure unit. They'd often been through the system – children's homes and foster homes – already. We were very much the 'last-chance saloon' for these unfortunates, our aim being to give them lots of love and firm boundaries, and in so doing improve their behaviour enough for them to be returned, not to their families – that option was mostly long gone – but to mainstream foster carers. That was what had just happened with Ashton and Olivia. So this situation was odd.

'That sounds unusual,' I told John.

'Even more than you know, Casey. This kid – whose name is Spencer, by the way – is only eight, yet he took himself off to social services on his own – just marched into their offices and demanded that they put him into care.'

'What?' I said, laughing incredulously. 'So he goes in there, asks for a foster carer and that's it? Is that what you're saying?'

'Well, not exactly. This actually happened a few weeks ago. And was taken seriously, too. There was a suspicious-looking bruise on his wrist, which he wasn't really able to account for – and neither was the father. Seems there's some sort of question mark in that regard about the mum. Anyway, naturally, it's all been followed up. Social services, family support and so on. They've been trying to support the family, offering coping strategies and advice, but none of it appears to have worked so far. There are five children in the family, little Spencer being the third of them, and there don't seem to be any issues or problems with the others. Mum's being treated for depression, apparently, but, bar this one child, the family *are* coping. Just not with Spencer. So that's where we are now.'

'Can't cope with him? Why ever not? You say he's eight, yes?'

'That's right.'

'So what could an eight-year-old have possibly done that's so bad?'

'Not that much, from what I can see, except that they've described him as almost feral. Had a yearning for the streets from a very young age. Running away all the time, even spending whole nights missing, and the parents say they simply don't know what to do with him any more. So now it's turned on its head, really. It's them who are pressing, because they don't feel confident they can keep him safe any more.'

'Bloody hell, John. That sounds crazy. That young and they can't keep control of him?'

'That's the story. And from what social services tell me, that really is the case. The other kids all appear absolutely fine.'

'So has he got mental-health problems? Psychological problems? What?'

'I'm told not. The parents apparently told social services that they are at a loss themselves. They described him as vicious and abnormal, and claim he was born evil.'

I balked at that. Honestly! Some people. Children weren't born evil. I truly believed that. They got damaged by environment, circumstances, neglect. It was that which caused behaviour to spiral out of control. Not some 'evil' gene. I'd yet to meet a child who was 'born bad'. I suspected I never would, either.

'Okay,' I said. 'And just when did you have in mind for this "evil" child to come to us?'

'Well, obviously, you'll want to speak to Mike first,' John answered. 'But if you're both in agreement, we could bring him over to meet you next Monday, with a view to him moving in that same week.'

Ah, I thought. Mike. Then I tried not to think it, as the last words my husband had said to me that morning were how much he was looking forward to a few weeks of peace. Just the two of us. A proper recharge of our batteries, after what by anyone's yardstick had been a rollercoaster of a year. 'And tonight,' he'd said, 'don't do a thing about dinner. I'm ordering in a takeaway, a nice bottle of your favourite wine, a few candles …'

Oh dear, I thought. Oh *dear*.

John went on to explain that Spencer was currently staying with another specialist carer temporarily. Her name was Annie and I knew her vaguely. She was in her mid-fifties, and I seemed to remember hearing on the grapevine that she'd recently lost her husband, poor thing. Because of this, and the fact that she was considering retirement soon anyway, she had asked to be considered only as a respite carer now; just stepping in when full-time foster carers needed a few days' break. Which was why, John finished, it was important they move Spencer on quickly. I could almost hear him crossing his fingers.

'Hmm,' said Riley once I'd put down the phone, having promised John I'd get back to him the following morning. 'I wouldn't like to be in your shoes when Dad gets home, for sure. What happened to the plan to take the rest of the summer off? Flown out of the window now, has it?'

I bustled us both back into the kitchen and winked at her as I took my coffee. 'Oh, you know me,' I said. 'Dad can always be persuaded …'

'Well, rather you than me,' she said. 'And Dad's right, Mum. With a job like this I think you *should* have a bit of a break before the next shock –'

'Shock? Honestly, Riley you make it sound so dramatic. They're only kids, you know, not little savages!'

Riley didn't need to answer, because even as I said it I was reminded that when Ashton and Olivia had arrived with us, little savages were exactly what they looked like.

Literally. More as if they'd strolled out of a prehistoric cave – all rags and lice and scabies – than from a council house an hour and a half's drive away.

But if I spent the rest of the day optimistically planning my strategy to break the news to him gently, I was soon to be reminded that it was going to be a tough one. It had been a glorious afternoon, most of which we'd spent out in the garden, and when David, Riley's partner, arrived to pick the family up, almost the first words she said to him were, 'You'll never guess what. Big, big news! Mum's only agreed to take on a new kid, like, next *week*. And without asking Dad.'

As with Riley's earlier, David's expression said it all. 'No, I haven't!' I protested. 'I haven't agreed to anything.'

Riley grinned and touched a finger to her temple. 'Yeah, you have,' she said, laughing. 'So good luck.'

Back inside and tidying the toys away, I smiled to myself. Riley knew me too well. Knew how much I'd want to do this. It was exactly the sort of challenge I loved. Just eight years old and already branded so horribly. It almost beggared belief, and I wanted to know more. I tidied the toys away, washed up the few plates and cups we'd used, then swept the floor and wiped down all the kitchen surfaces. I loved to clean. So much so that in my past life I think I must have been a scullery maid, but even with my exacting standards of housewifery the fact was that it wasn't six yet and I had nothing left to do. I couldn't even busy myself by making a start on dinner, because Mike was going to order in that takeaway. *See*, I told myself, *that's why I don't want a break. I'm bored. I have nothing to do all day now that the kids have left home. What else can I do if I don't have kids in?*

This was key. As a specialist carer, one of the conditions of my employment was that I didn't take any other job. I was required to be on call 24/7, as most of the kids we got in were so challenging, and needed such a lot of one-to-one support. Which was what I loved. Prior to fostering I'd been a behaviour manager in a large comprehensive school, looking after all the difficult and troubled kids. And it had been the idea of this demanding one-on-one role that had inspired me to do our kind of fostering in the first place.

*See*, I told myself again, popping out to the conservatory for a cigarette. I *needed* to have kids in. Without that challenge I just felt so redundant.

Having convinced myself that Mike would understand, I went back inside, grabbed the book I'd bought in town and started half-heartedly reading the first few pages. But I was barely taking in the words and was happy to fling it on the sofa as soon as I heard the sound of Mike's car.

'Hi, babes – how was your day?' I gushed, planting a kiss on his cheek as he walked into the hall. He was carrying the promised wine in one hand, and a big bunch of red roses – my favourite – in the other. 'Oh!' I cried, feeling even more guilty than ever. 'They're gorgeous. What an unexpected pleasure! Come on, let me put the kettle on and make you a nice mug of coffee.'

'Casey,' he said, his eyes narrowing. 'What have you done? Have you been out buying handbags? Come on. Own up.'

'Oh, for goodness sake, love,' I trilled. 'You're so suspicious. Can't I even be nice to you without you thinking there's an ulterior motive?'

His expression remained the same. 'Er … no. Not this nice.'

I flicked on the kettle and pulled a vase from the cupboard. 'Honestly,' I said, feigning great offence. 'That's so not fair. Though … um … I do have something I need to ask you.'

I had hoped this might sound like something of an unrelated afterthought, but my husband, who knew me as well as my kids did, was not fooled in the least.

'Here we go,' he said, plonking himself down at the kitchen table while I fussed about unwrapping the flowers and trying not to blush. 'Go on, then,' he finished. 'Let's have it.'

So I told him pretty much everything John had told me, gently skimming over the 'born evil' section, and making a great deal of the 'oh, I'm soooo bored' part.

Then I held my breath, waiting for the verdict. Which wasn't quite as immediately understanding as I'd hoped.

'Oh, Casey, *please* love. Not yet,' Mike said, with genuine feeling. 'It's only been two bloody minutes since the dog left home, let alone the last two kids. Can't we have a bit of a breather? Isn't there someone else who could take this on?'

I knew he had a point. It really had only felt like two minutes. And though I missed Bob – he was our son Kieron's dog, and had now gone to live with him and his girlfriend Lauren, at her parents – I knew the point that Mike was making was that for the first time in over two decades we had no one and nothing to worry about bar ourselves. There were the grandchildren, of course, but in terms of our home life … well, it was a first, and I could see what he was saying.

But I was on a mission and there was no way I was going to give up so easily. I had the bit between my teeth now. This child needed me. And having no one to worry about, to my mind, was overrated. Mike had his job as a warehouse manager, which involved some long hours, I understood that – but what was *I* supposed to do? I tried tugging, very gently, on his heart strings.

'So you're saying no?' I asked, sorrowfully. 'Is that it? I have to tell John they'll have to just dump him in a children's home?'

'That's not fair, Case,' he said levelly. 'And don't use words like "dump" on me, either. You know who I'm thinking about here. *You*. I'll be at work,' he pointed out. 'It's you that'll have to cope. And I seem to remember it wasn't too long ago that you were telling me just how much you were looking forward to being able to have a great deal more quality time with your own grandchildren.'

'I know,' I said, stabbing the stems into the vase distractedly. 'But I can do both. It's just one little boy, Mike. And I'm so bored. I really am –' He raised one eyebrow. 'Well, I soon will be, anyway. You *know* that. I can't rattle around here with nothing to do. I'll go stir crazy …'

'And what about our holiday? I thought we were going to have a few days away?'

'We still can. There's respite, don't forget.' I put down the stem I was holding, and crossed the kitchen. I put the wine bottle in the fridge – it would need chilling, after all – then I went back to the table and sat on his knee. With me at five foot nothing and Mike at six foot three, it was one of the few ways I could look him in the eye, on his level. 'Will you just think about it?' I asked him. 'Please? Anyway, we don't need a holiday. Look out of the window. It's just gorgeous. We can sunbathe in the garden. Pretty please?'

His eyes narrowed again, but I could see it was a different kind of narrowing. One that said 'here we go' as opposed to 'no, you don't'.

'You're not going to let this drop,' he said. 'Are you?'

'What do you think?' I answered.

Job done.

In the end we had a Mexican, drank the whole bottle of wine and watched an old favourite movie of ours, *American Werewolf in London*. 'Well, you did say this lad's a bit feral,' Mike quipped. 'So we can look upon this as a bit of prior research.'

Thematically, though, perhaps it should have been *Apocalypse Now*, for it signalled the end of our 'peace and quiet' time, for sure. But I didn't mind. I went to bed that night feeling a very happy bunny. I couldn't wait to see what Monday had in store.

# Chapter 2

I decided I would spend the rest of the weekend trying to be extra nice to Mike, as a thank you. Now he'd agreed we could take Spencer – provided the meeting went well, at any rate – I was fizzing with energy and excitement.

'Morning, love!' I trilled brightly, as I perched on the edge of the bed, bearing a tray groaning under the weight of a full English breakfast.

Mike stretched and eyed the tray of food suspiciously. I'd let him have a sleep in while I'd sneaked downstairs to cook it, and had been surprised that the smell of bacon frying hadn't already woken him.

'I've already agreed we can meet Spencer,' he said. 'So what is it –' he met my eye – 'that you're after *now*?'

'Honestly,' I said, crossing the room to fling open the curtains and let in the sunshine. 'I'm just being nice, okay, grumpy drawers! Look, I've made all your favourite things for you, as well. Even those fancy sausages with bits in that you like.'

He nodded. 'I can see that. So, go on, what *are* you after?'

I grinned. 'Well, I was thinking, since it's *such* a lovely day, that we should, I don't know, go out somewhere, maybe.'

'As in where?' he said, picking up his cutlery and tucking in.

'Oh, I don't mind. Anywhere you like, love,' I answered. 'Just a day trip. You know me. As long as there are some shops, I don't mind.'

'Ah,' he said, spearing a piece of sausage and waggling it, 'what you *really* mean, then, is that you'd like me to take you shopping to buy stuff for a kid that we haven't even met yet. Am I right?'

'Well ...'

Mike laughed. 'Honestly, love,' he said, 'never become a con-woman. Subterfuge is not one of your finer attributes.'

So I was busted. But I didn't care, because for all his sarky comments Mike was happy enough with my plan. So we drove to a pretty village about 20 miles away, had a walk and a lovely pub lunch, then hit the gorgeous little high street, which was full of two of my favourite things, charity shops and toy shops. So while Mike, bless him, trudged uncomplainingly behind me, I was able to pick up bargains galore.

At eight, Spencer was only a little younger than Ashton, our last boy, so I worked on the basis that he would probably enjoy similar things. I bought a pile of books, some

Lego, new jigsaws and a few puzzles, as well as restocking the box of craft items I liked to keep in the house. And though he raised his eyebrows on more than one occasion, Mike refrained from passing judgement on my probably over-the-top haul.

And to my delight, the rest of the family indulged me as well. On the Sunday (so much for living the quiet life once your kids leave …) we had the whole family over for a big roast. Kieron and Lauren, Riley and David, plus my two gorgeous grandsons, all of whom seemed happy to accept the reality that I was always at my happiest when I had a child to look after, however much of a challenge that child might turn out to be.

'Mind you,' commented Kieron as we sat down at the table, 'have you noticed how differently she does it these days, sis? You remember how she was when I pinched that lolly when I was little? How she dragged me back to the shop and made me give it back and apologise in front of everyone? And then I got grounded as well?'

'Quite right, too!' I chipped in.

'Yeah, Mum …' He lifted a finger to forestall me. 'But imagine if one of these foster kids did that. Oh no, it would be all, "*Oh, dear me, that's not acceptable behaviour. I'm afraid you lose ten points today, dear.*"'

Riley snorted. 'So this is since Mum became Scottish, then, is it?'

I laughed too. Whenever Kieron did a 'Mum' impersonation, for some reason he always made me sound just like Miss Jean Brodie, adopting this bizarre, high-pitched, Scottish twang. 'Hey, you two, don't mock, okay?' I retorted through my giggles. 'I *have* to do that. It's called guidelines, and I have to follow them. It's not the same as with your own kids.'

We were all falling about laughing, but this, in fact, was true. Where I'd come down like a ton of bricks with my own two when they were little – that was what parenting was all about, wasn't it? – it was different with children who had profound behaviour issues, and who were way past the point where being marched round to apologise to someone would be of any benefit at all. Indeed, for some kids it would be counter-productive. These kids needed a whole different approach if they were to make progress. And a structured one, of the kind we'd been trained to deliver. The children would indeed earn points for good behaviour, and once they'd earned them they could then spend them on privileges. It was all about modifying their behaviour to make it acceptable, and in such a way that they could see the benefit in this. If they did as they were asked they would enjoy a nicer life. It really was as simple a lesson to learn as that. And when delivered within an environment that was warm and supportive, the programme was so far proving to be a great success.

And that was what it sounded like this little boy needed, I mused, as, before going to bed that night, I popped in to open Spencer's bedroom window and fluff up the pillows on the bed I had already made up. Love and boundaries. We could certainly give him that while we had him. Though I'd obviously have to watch out for that comedy Scottish accent.

* * *

For all my excitement, I was still nervous when I woke up on Monday morning. Didn't matter how much I looked forward to getting these foster kids, there was always that anxiety about the first meeting with them because you never knew what to expect. The child could absolutely hate you from the start, or you'd click; you'd make a connection at that point or you wouldn't. Not that I worried unduly. Spencer was our fifth child now, so the one thing I did know was that I didn't find it difficult to put feelings aside. As a foster carer your *job* was to put differences aside, to care for the children you took on regardless of how they were towards you, and get on with the job at hand. Luckily, so far, though it had been rocky in places, I'd formed a strong attachment with the previous children we'd looked after. I hoped today was to be no exception.

Mike was also a little bit nervous. I could tell. He'd taken the morning off so we could meet Spencer together, and my plan was to be that after a quick slice of toast we'd give the house a once-over before our visitors arrived. But he was having none of it. 'For goodness sake, Case!' he snapped. 'The whole house is bloody spotless. Can you put down the Mr Sheen and just chill till they get here? Polishing the grain off the bloody banisters won't make them get here any sooner.'

I knew better than to argue at such a sensitive time, so I reluctantly put my duster away. And they were on the door-step not half an hour later anyway. It was what I'd come to expect as the usual posse. I ushered them all into the dining room for the meeting, and John Fulshaw, our link worker, made the introductions. There was Glenn Gallagher,

Spencer's social worker, and his temporary carer, Annie, and last but not least there was Spencer himself, half hidden by his carer and looking terrified.

'Hello sweetie,' I said to him, proffering my widest smile. 'Goodness, you're a big boy for eight.' Despite his nervousness, I could immediately see that this went down well – being called 'big', in my experience, always did with boys of his age. He looked sweet, too. A poppet. Not at all what I'd imagined, with a silky mop of toffee-coloured hair and eyes that went with it. Amber and melting, heavily lashed and wide. But as well as being cute he also looked fit. A solid lad, who looked a little bit older than his years. Well nourished and, at least superficially, well cared for.

'Hi, Mrs Watson,' he answered shyly.

'Oh, call me Casey,' I told him. I pointed. 'And this is Mike, okay?' I could see as they shook hands that Mike's first impression was the same as mine. That, like me, he had warmed to this sweet little boy. And he was polite too, carefully pulling a chair out for his carer, Annie, and waiting to be asked before sitting down himself. And when I poured tea and coffee and offered him milk and biscuits, he immediately asked her permission. 'Would that be okay?' he asked. A good sign.

'Of course, love,' she said. 'And then after you've had them, perhaps Mike could take you on a tour of the house, eh?'

So far, I thought, so not at all what I'd expected. Where on earth was this evil, feral child we'd been expecting? In fact, the start of the meeting went so well and so chattily that it began to seem surreal that this child was in care.

There was lots of laughter too, as Glenn went through a few of Spencer's likes and dislikes, even joshing with him: 'Oh, and by the way, Spencer particularly *loves* sprouts. Don't you, mate?' Spencer wrinkled up his nose in disgust.

'So,' said John, finally. 'How about that tour, then? Okay, Mike?'

'Absolutely,' Mike agreed, rising from the table. 'C'mon, lad,' he said to Spencer. 'Let me show you and Glenn around.'

But perhaps I should have sensed something. Because it was only a matter of seconds before the atmosphere changed completely, Annie turning in her seat to speak to John directly. 'Now then,' she said, looking agitated. 'You do know that I need to know today, don't you?' It took me a second to work out what she was talking about. But it soon became clear. 'That was the deal, you remember? If they don't want him –' she had the grace to glance in my direction as she said this – 'then you do understand I'm not prepared to wait for you to find someone else, don't you?'

I was shocked. And so, I think, was John. We all knew Spencer's placement with Annie was only temporary, but she seemed almost aggressive about demanding to be shot of him. 'Annie, you know today's only an introductory meeting,' John said levelly. 'And I certainly never promised you an answer today. Casey and Mike have only agreed to *consider* it.'

Annie heaved a decidedly heavy sigh. 'Look, I'm sorry,' she said, addressing me now, 'I know I shouldn't be pushing, but I really can't cope with kids like this any more. Years ago, then fine. But these days I'm on my own, and sadly ...' She finished then, punctuating her words with a resigned shrug.

'Look,' I said, 'I don't want to seem presumptuous, but, well, he seems okay to me. I mean he's obviously on his best behaviour, but the real child always ...'

'Oh, don't let his "little angel" act fool you!' she answered, her tone sharp. 'This kid, believe me, is one of a kind. He's like no kid I have *ever* met before in my life. No, *honestly*,' she added, obviously seeing my sceptical expression, 'I can't begin to try and describe what I mean, but there's definitely something not right about him, trust me.'

This brought me slightly up short. I'd had as much said to me before. About Justin, the first boy we'd ever fostered. And we'd done well to heed the warning. Though everything worked out in the end, we'd certainly been through the mill with him. But if that was the case with Spencer, so be it. Annie didn't know it, of course, but her words made no difference. I'd decided to take him the minute I saw him. And I was 99 per cent sure Mike felt the same. Even so, it was good – and I braced myself mentally – to have some insight that was not at first apparent.

The others came back then, and we rounded off the meeting by gathering a little more logistical info. We were told Spencer's likes and dislikes, and that he attended a special school that was geared to children who had difficulties in the 'mainstream'. I knew what this meant, from the years I'd spent in education myself. It was flowery language to describe an institution for the sort of kids who'd been kicked out of regular schools, and probably more than one, too. I glanced at John. We didn't comment. We didn't need to.

But even with that knowledge on board, I just couldn't believe that inside this child lurked a little monster. Once again, as he left, he was unfailingly polite, thanking us both for having him and saying how nice it was to meet us. 'An' I really hope you decide to let me live here,' he finished, 'cos I love that bedroom and your enormous big telly.'

'He seems fine,' whispered Mike as we stood on the doorstep and waved the car off.

'I know,' I whispered back. 'He's just so cute. Are you thinking what I'm thinking?'

'You even need to ask me?'

So we didn't make Annie wait. We called John back the same afternoon. We'd happily take him off her hands the following Monday.

# Chapter 3

Spencer's suitcase was bulging.

Which was something that immediately struck me as symbolic. The last kids we'd fostered had arrived with barely anything; just a tatty old bin bag containing clothes that looked like rags. Yet the battered, broken doll that had also been buried in there was as precious to little Olivia as would be any other cherished toy. The luggage a child came with, as I was fast learning, spoke volumes – the things a child dragged from placement to placement meant everything to them. Be it a favourite photograph, a special toy, or a crumpled letter from a loved one, these belongings were often the only attachment a child had, and gave them a sense that they were still a part of something wider than the place where they had currently ended up.

'Good grief, Spencer!' Glenn exclaimed, as he dragged the case over the doorstep. 'Come on, own up. You've smuggled the kitchen sink into here, haven't you?'

Spencer glanced up at me as if expecting to be repri-manded. 'I got *lots* of stuff,' he explained. 'But it's mostly just my trainers and all my games for the DS that's making it heavy.'

I didn't know what a DS was, and said so. Spencer oblig-ingly got the portable game console out of his backpack to show me, while Glenn commented that of all the things in Spencer's life this was the one thing he couldn't live without.

I smiled and nodded while he shyly showed me all the things it could do, but it was an indicator that I'd been at this job for a while now that my immediate thought was a cynical one: this would be my bargaining tool. Sad though it was, to be able to modify the behaviour of challenging children, such a tool was your most potent weapon. It was the things they loved most that they would be most moti-vated to stay in line for, so the DS would soon have a subtle change in status. Spencer would have to see it as a privilege and not a right.

But that was for writing into Spencer's behaviour plan, not for today. Today was all about welcoming him to our family, and trying to quell his understandable anxiety.

And he did look terribly anxious today. Because my kitchen and dining room were separated only by an arch-way and an island of worktops, I could keep an eye on things while everybody settled at the dining table, and I rustled up the drinks and biscuits. It had become some-thing of a ritual, this, I realised, since I'd begun fostering. The dining-table meetings and the round of refreshments, the wide-eyed child, the various official adults, the slight edge of formality. I watched Spencer take his seat beside Glenn, his social worker, and how he pulled it close enough so that the two of them were almost touching. I also noticed he had something in his hand that I'd not seen at first. Perhaps he'd pulled it out of his pocket.

'Who's this, then?' I asked him, as I brought the tray of coffees in, plus the usual array of biscuits, which he eyed but didn't touch. Close up I could see it was a glove puppet.

'Fluffy Cow,' he said. Which seemed apt. That's what it was.

'Fluffy Cow is Spencer's favourite toy, isn't it, mate?' Glenn explained. 'He likes to take it to bed with him, don't you?'

I could see Spencer stiffen slightly. 'I don't play with it or owt,' he said. 'It just stays on my bed.'

'Of course,' I said. 'Here, love. Help yourself to a biscuit. And I tell you what, we've got to do a whole load of boring paperwork. So how about you take Fluffy Cow up to see your new bedroom? There's some new toys up there for you, so you might like to have a little play. But only if you want to,' I finished. 'It's entirely up to you.'

Spencer looked at Glenn. 'You won't go or anything, will you?'

'Course not, son,' he said. 'And I'll give you a shout if we need you.'

'Okay, then,' said Spencer, sliding back down off his chair and, clutching his beloved puppet, slipping noise-lessly from the room.

Bless him, I thought. Poor little lad. I really, really couldn't fathom this.

\* \* \*

The file Glenn handed out was a small one. Small but to the point. It made for grim reading. Spencer, as we'd known, was the middle of five children. He had a brother, Lewis, who was ten, a sister, Sammy Lee, nine, then two younger siblings, five-year-old Coral and a three-year-old called Harvey. Their parents, Kerry and Danny, were both in their thirties and apparently had no misgivings about Spencer coming into care. In fact, they'd been clear on this when they'd been interviewed by social services. As things stood they had decided to wash their hands of him. They said he was out of control, wild and 'feral' – that damning word again – and that they considered him to be a risk to both himself and others, and that they felt they'd reached the end of the road.

As was usual, a risk assessment had also been completed, and the finding was that as Spencer was a persistent petty offender priority had to be given to minimising his chances of re-offending and heading towards a life of teenage crime.

Once again, I was struck by the disparity between what I was reading and what I was seeing. I also wondered, as I read on, what kind of parents would feel able to hand over one of their five children to what could only be described as complete strangers, whether sanctioned by the council or otherwise. Why this 'one bad apple' attitude, that seemed to permeate through the paperwork? Were they worried that if he stayed he might 'infect' his brothers and sisters? How could you make such a chilling judgement about your own flesh and blood?

I glanced around the table as I finished reading, and John caught my eye. His expression was sad, and I could see he felt the same as me.

He shook his head slightly and slowly took off his reading glasses. These were new, and I made a mental note to compare notes with him about them later. I had just started needing to use them myself. 'Well, there's not an awful lot here, is there?' he said, pointing to the file. 'But what we do have makes it clear that Mr and Mrs Herrington, here, seem to think we can wave some sort of magic wand, sort their kid out and hand back some new, improved version, don't they?'

Glenn nodded. 'I got that impression too. Though I think – well, I *hope* – they now realise it's really not that simple. That said, the plan is still to do that, pretty much. A few weeks or months with Mike and Casey on the behavioural programme, and lots of visits home so they can actually see progress. Then overnights, then weekends, then – well, all being well, we'll have the family reunited at the end of it.'

I glanced at John again. 'Oh,' I said. 'So he's to do the full programme then, is he? You do realise that could take up to a year.'

'Well, not exactly,' John said. 'The intention is obviously to get him back home as soon as possible. I was thinking he could do a more scaled-down version of the programme, focusing mainly on his behaviour, and leaving out all the day-to-day mundane stuff, because it seems clear there's not much point in a child like him *earning* points from brushing his teeth and putting his dirty laundry in the right place.'

'Ahem?' I said pointedly.

John rolled his eyes at me. He knew full well he was being wound up. 'I mean obviously he'll still be expected to *do* all those things. Just not earn privileges by doing them, was what I meant to say.' I nodded, satisfied. 'Which means it'll be more intense, of course,' he finished, 'but hopefully that bit faster to implement. After all, he's young, compared to most of the kids we put on the programme, so I'm hoping we'll be able to nip things in the bud and turn him around.'

This was a fair point. The older the child was, the more ingrained their behaviours tended to be, and since older kids invariably came with more emotional baggage too (particularly if they'd spent a long time in care) it was a more complex business all round. Spencer was different. He'd only just come into the care system, so John's thinking would hopefully turn out to be sound. And yet, for all that, he had still been cast as an outsider – by everyone around him, by all accounts. He was so young but had already been disowned by his parents, had a history of petty offences and was a pupil at a special school. How had this young boy managed to get to this place, when the rest of his family were essentially so sound? It didn't stack up. Quite where was this monstrous child? There must be a lot more going on here than I could see.

We spent another 15 minutes or so going through the rest of the paperwork, and throwing around a few ideas about how to tailor the programme to suit Spencer, then Glenn called him down to say his goodbyes. He looked no less anxious as he came down the stairs to say farewell, and it was clear that even in the short time they'd been acquainted they seemed to have quite a rapport. This was a bonus, as our paths would cross often during this process, and it helped enormously if Mike and I had a rapport with him too.

And there was plenty to like. In his late 20s, I estimated, Glenn seemed both positive and enthusiastic, two qualities that a career in social services could often extinguish all too quickly. You saw too much that you wished you hadn't, had to make too many difficult decisions and worked in a sector that could often be thankless; damned if you took a child away, and damned if you didn't. Spencer was fortunate, I thought, to have Glenn on side. And though professional in approach, he also *looked* approachable. With his jeans and his shades and his cool designer T-shirts, he was the sort of character that kids wouldn't be intimidated by, which would help them open up to him, which mattered.

And it wasn't just Glenn who had an eye for designer kit. When I went upstairs with Spencer to help him with his unpacking, the first things I saw were five pairs of expensive-looking trainers, all pristine and laid in a neat row against the wall.

'Wow, I said. 'Look at these. You certainly like your trainers, don't you?'

Spencer nodded. 'I love 'em. But I only wear this make, because this make's the coolest.' He looked at me anxiously, then. 'Mrs Watson?'

'It's Casey, love. Casey and Mike, I told you.'

'Erm, Casey?' he asked anxiously. 'You know you mustn't put them in the washing machine don't you? Or they'll get ruined.'

I grinned. 'Message received and understood. And don't worry, love. My son Kieron – you'll meet him in the next day or two – he's pretty pernickety about his stuff, as well, so I've had lots of practice.'

He looked relieved at this. 'Glenn said you had other kids. Does he live here?'

I shook my head as I began helping him unpack his clothes, all of which, unusually, were good quality. 'Both my children are grown-up now,' I explained, 'though they live nearby. One of them – my daughter Riley, who you'll meet too – even has two little ones of her own. Just a little younger …' I caught the words before they had a chance to run away from me. This was definitely not the time to start mentioning his younger siblings. Time for that later. Right now, it would probably only upset him. '… than the last little girl we had to stay with us,' I quickly improvised. 'Talking of which,' I added. 'Her favourite thing in the whole wide world was pizza. So how about you? If you could have anything you wanted – anything in the world – for your tea tonight, what would it be?'

He seemed to consider for a moment, tapping his finger against his lip. 'I don't mind,' he said eventually. 'Anything is fine.'

I shook my head. 'No it isn't. Come on, think.'

'I don't mind, really.'

My heart went out to him. It was obviously proving difficult for him to express a preference, because he'd been taught that that wouldn't be polite. He was such a mystery, this little boy, this apparent 'monster' in our midst, and I wondered quite when we'd be seeing him.

By now we'd almost finished putting away all his clothes, and I was struck again, seeing how carefully he folded them all, at how he seemed so unlike any child in the care system I'd come across; my end of the care system, anyway.

'I'm afraid I insist,' I said, mock-sternly. 'It's part of the rules. You tell me all the things you like, and then I cook them. No point giving you things to eat that you don't like, is there? So. We already know about how much you love sprouts, don't we? So as soon as they're in the shops, I'll get lots of them in …'

This seemed to do it. 'Meatballs with spaghetti?' he suggested, blinking at me nervously. 'I really like them …'

'Perfect,' I said. 'Because that's Mike's favourite too. And that's with sprouts, then, is it?'

At which he finally cracked a smile.

The day continued in a similarly positive vein. Mike had gone into work for a couple of hours and I was happy enough to let Spencer play on his computer games for a while, and also rigged up the PlayStation for him. I knew people worried about kids spending too much time glued to screens these days, and I certainly accepted whatever evidence there was, but at the same time I didn't hold with the often-touted line that this kind of media was always the enemy. In my experience, new kids always seemed to settle better when allowed access to favourite computer games. They needed to be age-appropriate, obviously, but I saw more good than harm in them having some 'down time' of this kind. It really did seem to help kids calm down, particularly if they bordered on the hyperactive. Many games also had positive educational benefits, helping kids focus and concentrate.

Whatever the intellectual debates about it, when Mike returned home from the warehouse Spencer seemed a lot more relaxed. He was also less timid now, and a pleasure to sit and chat to, and he turned out, as we sat around the table and ate the spaghetti and meatballs, to be very knowledge-able about football. Which was brilliant, because football loomed large in the Watson family. Both Mike and Kieron loved it and Kieron played it, too. The ritual of Mike going to watch him play every Saturday was one of those commit-ments that were pretty much set in stone.

The only snag was that Spencer turned out to be a fan of Aston Villa, whereas Mike was a dyed in-the-wool Leeds fan. This naturally resulted in a more heated discussion, in which a string of not very nice names were applied to a long list of people I had never heard of.

'I think I'll just clear the table and start the washing up,' I said, as Mike pointed out to Spencer all the reasons why some player on one of their teams should not have done this, that or the other, and Spencer came back with an equally measured argument about why, in this case, Mike was wrong.

The net result was that both of them completely failed to hear me, so I gathered the plates and took them back into the kitchen. I didn't mind. There was nothing Mike enjoyed more than a bit of banter about football around the tea table, something he'd really missed since Kieron had left home. And it sounded as if Spencer really knew his stuff, too.

*Too Hurt to Stay*

I smiled as I began filling the sink and rolled my sleeves up. I knew how the adage went. 'No smoke without fire.' And I wasn't stupid, either. Little Spencer, delightful as he had seemed to be so far, was living under my roof for a reason. But right now, much as I was braced for whatever was coming, I couldn't feel anything but positive about him. Just how bad could this boy possibly be?

# Chapter 4

Wherever this apparent alter ego was hidden, Spencer clearly wasn't prepared to reveal it to us yet. In fact as the days went by he seemed to be turning into one of the best little house guests we'd ever had. Also, on the face of it, one of the sharpest, which in hindsight should perhaps have made me think.

He was an intelligent boy, and straight away he seemed keen to get to grips with the programme, the idea of which we had sketched out to him the day after he'd arrived. He was particularly fascinated with the whole system of points and levels, and keen to study what he had to do to earn privileges.

'Right, then,' he said, one afternoon towards the end of the second week, while he was sitting in the kitchen with me, eating his lunch. 'So all I need is a hundred points a day, and then I get to watch TV, go on the PlayStation for half an hour and play on my DS.'

'Or,' I said. 'Not "and". It's "or". But, yes, that's right. And any points you get over the hundred can go towards extra things, like ordering a takeaway meal one night, or renting a movie. Things like that.'

He nodded, and continued to study the lists. There was one detailing how many points each given task was worth, and another detailing what they could 'buy'. I watched how intently he was studying them, his eyes darting back and forth, when he suddenly clapped a hand down on the kitchen table. 'Aha,' he said, a grin spreading across his innocent, cherubic face. 'So, hang on a minute … there's nothing here about losing points, is there? Is that right, Casey? I don't lose points for being naughty or anything? I just get to win points for the good stuff I do?'

He clearly wasn't interested in having a philosophical discussion about carrots versus sticks and their various merits. He'd spotted something. His expression made that clear. I didn't like the way this conversation seemed to be going. I thought about my answer before replying. 'Well, I suppose so,' I said, finally. 'But then again, if you were doing bad things, you wouldn't be earning any points, would you?'

'I *could*!' he said, pointing emphatically at the piece of paper. 'If I clean my room, get ready for school – when I go back to school, anyway – then do two jobs around the house, and go to bed on time without moaning, that's almost my hundred points, there.' He grinned. 'So then all I'd have to do is to be polite and respectful to some adults and that's it! Even if I *did* do something bad, I would still have got my hundred points, wouldn't I? I mean I'm not going to *be* bad. I'm just saying.'

I stared at Spencer, who was looking as sweet and innocent as the day is long, and then I looked at the points sheet
and pondered. Here he was, an eight-year-old, trying to
work out how he could turn things – this entirely new situation – to his advantage, and at first glance he appeared to
be right. Surely there must be some mistake. I picked up
the points sheet and went through it in my mind. Incredible
to think that this had never come up before. Incredible to
think I'd never even thought it. And then I saw it. 'Hang
on a minute,' I said. 'Slow down a bit, Spencer. You *are*
right, in that you wouldn't *lose* the points you'd earned that
day. But if you *had* misbehaved on this example day you
talk about, then you wouldn't get the extra points, would
you?'

'Yeah, I would,' he said. I shook my head. He studied the
sheet too. 'Why not?'

I pointed to the item I'd identified on the sheet. 'Because
if you did something naughty, who would decide it was
naughty? An *adult*. Which means you wouldn't get the
showing respect points, would you? Because it isn't respectful of an adult's feelings if you misbehave, is it?'

Spencer took – in fact, almost snatched – the sheet from
my hand, so determined was he to prove me wrong. He
spent quite a while very obviously searching for a loophole,
before slapping it down again and picking up his sandwich,
thoroughly cross. 'Humph,' he said irritably, before he bit
into it. 'Well, it's not very clear, that chart, is it?'

I could have ticked him off for his cheek. In fact, it
almost made me laugh. Perhaps this was our first glimpse
of the real Spencer.

But on the whole he was the picture of perfection, and when Riley and the kids came to visit on the Saturday he even melted my heart a little at the way he was with Levi, who at almost three apparently reminded him of his little brother.

'Ooh,' he said, once introduced, 'you're just like my little Harvey. Do you wanna come and play with my dinosaurs with me? My Harvey loves dinosaurs.' He held out his hand and Levi wasted no time in taking it, seeming delighted at having someone new to play with.

Riley pulled out the toy box with the dinosaurs in it, to which Spencer had already added his own stash. Watching, I was taken by his willingness to share. And also his willingness to play with little Levi. Not every child, in my experience, was quite so friendly. It was so obvious he'd come from a home and not a 'home' – as in an institution-type home such as the one in which our first foster child had lived.

'That's really nice of you,' I said, as they hauled the box into the middle of the living room. 'Kind of you to play with Levi. Thanks, love.'

He smiled broadly. 'It's fine. I'll come and let you know when I get bored.'

'He seems lovely, Mum,' Riley commented as we went into the kitchen with the baby, leaving the living-room door open so we could still keep an eye on things. There seemed nothing to fear here, but our fingers had been burned; the sort of kids I fostered didn't always have the usual boundaries, as we'd found out more than once. 'Really sweet kid,' she continued, while I cooed over the baby. 'Shall I sort out some drinks and biscuits for them?'

'I'll get the milk,' I said, hoisting Jackson up onto my hip. 'You should find some Jaffa Cakes in the treats cupboard.'

She rummaged in my wall cupboard. 'Nope. There's half a packet of Jammie Dodgers though. They'll do.'

'You sure?' I asked, joining her. 'I definitely bought some. You know, I think I'm going mad. That's about the third time this week that I've gone to get something only to find it's not there.'

Riley laughed. 'That's just your age!'

I laughed as well, as she took the snacks in to the children, but it wasn't. It had happened the day before, too, when I'd bought home a new DVD. I'd looked everywhere – even double-checked the receipt, just to convince myself I'd actually bought it – but having put it down I'd not been able to find it anywhere. I'd asked Mike and I'd asked Spencer, but neither had seen it. And it had been the same with a pair of earrings I'd left by the bathroom basin. And now this. An unpalatable thought began taking shape in my mind.

Riley had now returned and we both sat down at the kitchen table. 'You know what?' I said, as I settled Jackson on my lap with his favourite squeaky duck. 'This isn't the first time something's gone missing this week.' I lowered my voice a little. 'Now I'm wondering if it's Spencer.'

'What, like stealing from you?'

'Maybe. Or maybe "borrowing". Or maybe as some sort of game. Who knows? Or maybe it *is* just my age. It's just … hmm, well, I think I'll have to keep my eye out, won't I?

It won't be the first time. These things do happen. Occupational hazard!'

We moved on then, changed the subject, and got on with catching up on gossip. And when Spencer finally tired of playing dinosaurs with Levi, as he'd predicted, we relocated to the living room so Levi could instead play with Jackson, who'd just started crawling. Well, a kind of crawling, anyway. It was actually more rolling and pulling himself about using his elbows, but it got him from A to B efficiently enough.

Spencer, at that point, went back up to his room, and the rest of the afternoon sped by. So much so that our loose plan to pop to the shops at some point had disappeared along with the Jaffa Cakes. That was often the way things worked out at the moment. One toddler was fine, one little baby was a breeze, but sometimes the business of getting kitted out, and then trailing both of them round town – with an eight-year-old boy in tow now too, for that matter – involved more effort than the pair of us felt like making, especially on what was turning out to be a typically wet late-August day. Spencer had also come back down to join us, and I'd put a Disney film on for them to watch.

We were still in the living room when Mike got home from watching Kieron playing football, and, shocked to find us there, he even commented on it. He picked up Levi and swung him up high over his head, causing Jackson to dissolve into fits of giggles. 'Now then, mister,' he asked, 'how come your mummy and your nanna aren't out shopping? It's incredible. Did you confiscate their purses?'

Unbeknown to Mike, he'd said something particularly astute, because 20 minutes later, after we'd packed away the toys ready for Mike to drop them home, Riley couldn't seem to lay hands on hers.

'You seen my purse, Mum?' she asked, following me out into the kitchen, rummaging in her handbag as she went. About to leave now, she wanted to pay me for some raffle tickets I'd been selling for a local charity, and had brought the money round especially.

'I haven't, love,' I said. 'You definitely sure you brought it?'

'Course I'm sure. Maybe Levi's been messing about with it. Levi,' she asked as he toddled in behind her, 'have you been playing with Mummy's purse?' He looked at her blankly, shaking his head. 'Spencer, how about you?' I asked, following Riley back into the living room to look for it. He was sitting where we'd left him, the movie still running, and there was something about his demeanour that made me look twice.

'No,' he said, chewing his nails. 'Why would I know anything about it? That's typical, that is. Why am *I* getting the blame? I always get the blame for what little kids do.'

A clear case, it occurred to me, of protesting too much. 'I'm not blaming you, Spencer. I was just asking if you'd seen it. Now can you help us look, please? Riley's due home and she needs to find her purse.'

He stood up quickly enough and I assumed he was going to help, but instead he made straight for the door and up the stairs. Moments later, we all heard his bedroom door slam.

'Well,' said Mike, who'd caught the tail-end of this, 'that was something of an over-reaction, don't you think?'

'It was,' I replied. 'And I wonder if there's more to it.'

I told him of my suspicions about the things that had gone missing. He didn't look surprised.

'Well, that's probably it, then,' he said. 'After all, they did say he had hidden depths, didn't they? So maybe that's it. Maybe that's what the petty offences all were. Maybe stealing's his thing.'

'God,' said Riley. 'Honestly …'

Mike frowned. 'Which means we'll have to search his room, of course.'

I felt hesitant. 'But what if it isn't him? What if that's exactly the sort of thing that happens to him at home? Won't make for much of a start, will it, making it clear we don't trust him?'

'Mum,' said Riley, 'I take your point, but it can really only have been *him*. If Levi had had it out we would have already found it, wouldn't we? He's not been anywhere else in the house today, has he? And I definitely had it, and he was in here all that time, *with* my handbag. It *must* have been him.'

'We need to confront him, at least,' Mike added. So, all out of options, we trooped up the stairs.

Mike knocked on the door before pushing it open, and found Spencer sitting on his bed, reading a book. 'Listen, mate,' Mike said, 'I know you said you hadn't moved Riley's purse, but when something goes missing we have no choice but to search everywhere for it, and that includes your room, I'm afraid. Is that okay?'

*Casey Watson*

Spencer shrugged and stood up. 'Course,' he said, moving into the doorway, out of the way. 'Help yourself. That's fine.' Mike began searching.

I joined him. Between us we found nothing. We looked under the bed, behind the curtains, under the pillows, inside the drawers. I'd been fostering long enough to have got pretty clever: our very first child, more chillingly, had a habit of self-harming, and used to carefully stash any sort of blade he could find. With Spencer watching, however, this felt distinctly uncomfortable, especially as it looked as though the purse really wasn't there.

'It's obviously not here, Mike,' I began, having run out of places to look for it. 'Let's go and have another look in the dining room, shall we? Perhaps it's –'

Mike raised an arm then, to stop me. He now had an odd sort of look on his face. And as I watched, his gaze moved from Spencer to the wall – to the place where we'd hung a print of two footballers. He held his gaze there, and the effect on Spencer was immediate. He let out a whimper, then suddenly rattled off down the stairs.

'What the … hey!' I heard Riley exclaim, from the hall. She was waiting there with the little ones, phoning David.

'What?' I asked Mike. 'What is it, love?'

'That picture.' He crossed the room in two strides and clasped the print in both hands, lifting it slightly so he could free the cord and take it off the wall.

I was just wondering how on earth you could hide a purse behind a picture – *any* purse, let alone Riley's receipt-stuffed great big thing – when the question I'd not yet

40

finished asking was answered. As Mike stepped back with it we both gasped in unison, unable to quite believe what we were seeing.

Before us was a hole, in the shape of a raggedy-edged circle, about eight inches in diameter and going back some way. Enough plaster had been dug out to expose the timber framework, and as I stepped closer it was clear that a huge space had been made available, because Mike was already beginning to pass things to me. First the Jaffa Cakes, unopened, then the missing DVD, then the earrings, which had been carefully wrapped in a folded envelope, then one of my necklaces – one that I hadn't even realised was missing – then a cigarette lighter Riley had accused me the week before of losing, then finally, with a last insertion of Mike's arm, Riley's purse.

I stood speechless with shock at the scene laid before me. If we'd found this stash anywhere else, I could have believed it. The bottom of the wardrobe, say, or tucked away in a box under the bed. But it was that hole. That painstakingly constructed hole had floored me. How much time, how much industry, how many handfuls of carefully smuggled plasterboard must have gone into the creation of that secret safe of his? He was eight years old. *Eight!* It seemed beyond comprehension. Except, was it?

Mike brushed plaster dust from his forearm and pulled his sleeve down. 'Well, we can't say we weren't warned,' he said.

# Chapter 5

'Right,' said Mike, his expression grim. 'This needs tackling right now.'

He laid the picture on the bed and we both trooped back down the stairs. At the bottom of them Jackson was now dozing peacefully in his push chair, but Riley had followed Spencer into the living room, Levi close behind her.

'He's behind the sofa,' she told Mike. 'Curled up in a ball. I've tried talking to him but he's not saying anything. I take it he did have my purse then?' she asked, turning to me. 'Whoah!' she exclaimed then, seeing the haul in my hands. 'My purse and then some.'

'Come on, young man,' Mike said, sternly pulling the sofa out a little. 'Out from there, please. We need an explanation for this, mate. You can't just go taking things that don't belong to you.'

But Spencer had no intention of coming out, it seemed. In response to Mike's words he just made himself even smaller, hands over his ears, head pressed into his knees, rocking back and forth as if trying to block the world out. A not untypical reaction from a boy of his age, I mused. Not when they've been caught red handed.

'Come on, love,' I coaxed. 'We just need to talk about it, that's all. You don't need to take things, love. If there's something you want, you only need to ask.'

I got glared at for this by both my husband and my daughter. I could even hear Riley's unspoken words: you want my purse and all the money in it? Yeah, of course, mate!

But I felt a softer approach would be the only one that would work here. 'Spencer,' I said. 'You can't stay here for ever, love, now, can you? Hiding away's not going to help. We need to discuss this.'

Riley's phone chimed. 'That's David,' she huffed. 'He must be outside. I have to go. Dad, can you help me with the kids, please? Leave Mum to deal with the Artful Dodger here, shall we?'

I almost smiled, but not quite. The image of that hole in one of my bedroom walls stopped me. But Spencer did look a little like he might have been recruited by Fagin. What with his mop of silky hair and his butter-wouldn't-melt looks. And a rather forlorn sight, right now – very Dickensian – as he trembled and cowed behind the sofa.

But I was wrong to be fooled by such superficial details.

'Come on, love,' I began, while Mike went out to help Riley transfer Jackson into his car seat, and stow the push chair in the boot of David's car. 'Come out and let's sit down and talk about this, eh?'

But I barely had time to finish what I was saying, because Spencer, apparently having decided the coast was clear – well, of Mike, anyway – was up out of his hidey hole and barging right past me. 'Fuck off!' he yelled. 'I'm off to bed and don't no one *dare* come up. I *hate you all*!' And there he was, gone.

*Ah*, I thought, as I watched him go. *And so the fun begins.* The real work, I knew, was about to start.

In the end, I decided to let Mike deal with him. Already he seemed to be a boy who responded to male authority, so Mike's suggestion – that Spencer would be more likely to realise how serious this was if the dressing down came from him – seemed a good one.

It was a full 20 minutes before Mike was back downstairs. 'Well, I don't know if it's done any good,' he said, 'but he did apologise.'

'And did he say why he'd done it?'

Mike shook his head. 'Just sat and listened to me, mostly,' he answered. 'Then said sorry, and that it wouldn't happen again. I did ask why he'd done it – that he must have known it was wrong – but he had no answer. Just said he didn't know.'

'Is he coming down for tea, then?' I asked, beginning to dish out the bolognaise that I'd finished preparing while Mike had been upstairs.

'On his way. I just told him to wash his face and hands and come straight down. Oh, and I did tell him that he wouldn't be getting all his behaviour points today, so no TV or DS tomorrow. He seemed to accept that.'

It seemed Mike was right. Spencer was quiet and a bit sullen looking as he sat and ate his tea, but I was at least pleased to see he looked chastened. And after tea, when he went back upstairs to play with his toy dinosaurs, we both agreed that, however destructive the hole-making and the stealing, it at least gave us a chance to see what we were dealing with, and a benchmark from which to improve.

But the sense of contrition wasn't destined to last long. At around nine, when Spencer came down for a drink and a biscuit, I decided I'd take the opportunity to have a quick run through his points with him, just so he knew how things stood. This was important. The whole point and reward system was new to him, and almost as important as the business of actually earning them was that the child make the connection between actions and consequences; that was the foundation on which the whole model was based.

At first, as I explained about the deficit and its conse-quences for privileges tomorrow, he seemed resigned and accepting. 'That's okay,' he said meekly. 'I know there'll be no TV time tomorrow.'

'And I'll also have to ground you. You do know that, too, don't you? So there'll be no playing out for the next few days.'

Though I'd mentioned it, I'd assumed this would be inconsequential – Spencer hadn't once yet *asked* to go out to play. But I couldn't have been more wrong. He almost harrumphed. 'What?' he said. 'I thought my punishment was no TV?'

'No, love. It's not your punishment. It's that you can't afford to *buy* it. You can't afford to buy TV time because you won't have enough points. If you did, then you'd still be able to buy TV time, wouldn't you? No, your punishment is not being allowed to go out to play. You know that. We went through all that at the start, remember?'

His expression hardened. 'But that's crap! That's like punishing me twice.'

I shook my head. 'Spencer, I don't even see why this is bothering you – you haven't been out to play. You've not even wanted to.'

He folded his arms across his chest. 'But I was going to! And now I can't. Is that what you're saying?'

It felt like I was talking to a tiny politician. A very cross one. 'Yes, love, it is,' I confirmed. 'For this week, at least.'

'God, that's so unfair!'

I was still shaking my head in disbelief as he stomped back off up the stairs, but as the days passed it became clear that this wasn't about playing out. For Spencer, it was a matter of principle. He simply wouldn't let it rest, mumbling to himself about it constantly, and going off on one about 'injustice' half a dozen times a day. By the time Wednesday came around and he was due back at school, I couldn't have been happier. Perhaps now we'd see the end of it.

But school, it seemed, was just another irritant in his life. Just another thing to ruin his day.

'I hate school,' he told me, after I'd nagged him about the time for the umpteenth time. 'And my teacher,' he added as he climbed into the back of the car.

'Oh, you'll be fine once you get there,' I said, wincing as he slammed the car door, for good measure. 'Once you see your friends again, you'll see. It's always a bit nerve-racking after the long summer holidays. But once you're back ... tell you what. Shall I put a CD on? Some music to take your mind off things maybe?'

This seemed to cheer him up. 'I've got one,' he said, brightening. 'Here.' He passed me a CD he'd fished out of his backpack. 'It's my favourite. It's the Chipmunks.'

It was, too. For the next 15 minutes all conversation was halted as he hummed along to some frankly bizarre, squeaky renditions of a bunch of pop songs I'd never even heard before. But it did seem to have worked, because as we turned into the school car park his mood seemed to have brightened considerably.

It was one of those balmy September days that just seem perfect for starting school again. Warm and golden, with just enough of an autumnal tinge to signal that summer's languid days were over and it was time to sharpen pencils and start work. It was a time of year I'd always loved; all crisp new uniforms and a clear sense of purpose. But, as I was about to find out, it was not a feeling Spencer shared.

The unit – the more correct name for what Spencer knew as school – was actually a large house, set in the middle of a ring of mature trees. It looked inviting and appealing; very much a place of learning, even though I knew that most of the children who attended it were there precisely because they all had challenges with doing just that. Not that it wasn't somewhat obvious. We entered via a pair of electronically opened gates, which began closing again immediately we passed through them.

I parked up, got out of the car and opened Spencer's door – he couldn't do it himself, because of the child lock – and, once I'd done so, leaned back in to the front passenger foot well to grab my handbag. It was then, to my astonishment, that he made what was obviously a bid for freedom, sprinting across the car park towards the now secured gates. It took mere seconds for him to scale them – he was obviously something of an expert – and even found time, as I hurried in pursuit, to give me the finger before jogging off down the road.

Happily, at that point, another car had pulled up and, as I watched from behind the now re-opening gates, the occupant jumped out, shouting, 'Don't worry! I'll catch him!' before sprinting off after his rapidly disappearing prey.

To say I was bemused would be an understatement. I was now standing in the middle of what looked like a crime scene: the gates swinging open, the car blocking the entrance, its driver's door still flung open, the dust that had been kicked up by the chase slowly settling. I was also, for all that, thinking fast. The man – who I presumed must be a teacher, and who looked to be in his late twenties – clearly knew exactly what he was dealing with. I'd also got the impression he knew where to go, and every confidence he'd bring his diminutive charge to heel.

But why hadn't *I* been told about this? Because from the evidence in front of me it seemed pretty clear that young Spencer was a serial absconder.

It was a good ten minutes before the two of them were once again in sight, walking towards me. 'What on earth was that about?' I asked Spencer, as soon as he was in earshot. 'You nearly gave me a heart attack. What were you *thinking*?'

The young man stuck a hand out and grinned at me amiably. 'Mr Gorman,' he said. 'Very nice to meet you. You'll be Spencer's foster mother, then, will you?'

I nodded and introduced myself. 'And I'm really, really sorry. I had no idea he'd try to run away. I'm so sorry.'

'Oh, don't worry, Mrs Watson,' he said. 'Not your fault. Someone should have told you – young Spencer here doesn't like our school a whole lot.' He playfully ruffled Spencer's hair. 'Isn't that right, young man?'

We started towards the entrance, Mr Gorman's hand gently guiding Spencer. 'His mum and dad used to have to physically bring him right into reception,' he said chattily. 'But he's always fine once he's in, aren't you, mate?'

Spencer looked resigned, but, at the same time, a little pleased with himself. There was clearly a bond here, and something else besides. This stunt of his had brought him some positive attention. Was that a part of why he did it? 'Come on,' said Mr Gorman, laughing. 'Let's get you settled in your class, then Mrs Watson and I can have a chat, okay?'

'Okay, sir,' Spencer answered. 'But it was worth a try though, wannit?' And with that, he skipped off to class, grinning cheekily.

\* \* \*

It took around 20 minutes for Mr Gorman to give me a quick guided tour of the school. He was Spencer's supervising teacher – a role that a head of year would have in a conventional school – and as we walked he told me Spencer was a miniature Houdini, who'd abscond any chance he could get. What the school did, he explained, was to minimise those chances, keeping him occupied almost every moment of the school day, and never letting him out into the grounds unsupervised. This was reassuring, though it did leave me very unnerved. At no point had anyone mentioned this to me or Mike before, much less given us any directives about keeping him indoors. Surely something like this should have come up? I made a mental note to ring the supervising social worker.

I was still ruminating on this as I drove round to Riley's, where I'd planned on spending much of the school day. Spencer was eight, much too young to be safe out alone. It seemed clear I'd need to keep my wits about me.

'Not that you'll be able to do a lot about it anyway,' said Riley, after I'd droned on for half an hour. 'I mean, you can obviously keep him indoors all the while he's grounded. But what about next week? You're going to have to let him out then, aren't you?'

'Am I? At eight? Unsupervised? That feels so young.'

Riley pointed towards her kitchen window, which looked out onto her street. 'Not at all. Just look out there at three thirty any weekday. There are kids way younger than eight playing out these days.'

God, I thought, as I drained my mug of coffee. This

placement might prove to be harder than I'd thought. I would need eyes in the back of my head.

I spent the rest of the day with Riley and the little ones, which worked its magic, as usual, and when I arrived back to collect him it seemed school had done likewise with Spencer. He ran out to me brandishing a picture he'd painted, obviously in very high spirits.

'It's for you and Mike,' he said proudly, as he held it up to show me. 'This is a mountain, an' that's the black sky – cos it's dark – an' this here, with all the red on, is a dead wolf. That's its blood an' guts all over that rock there,' he finished proudly. 'D'you like it?'

I nodded as I surveyed the colourful scene of bloody carnage. 'Very good – very *artistic*,' I agreed.

Mr Gorman was in high spirits too. I got the impression that every day he hung on to Spencer was a day for celebration. 'We've had a good day today, haven't we, Spencer?'

And it seemed we were going to have a good evening too. We played Lego after tea, and then Mike produced a new DVD, which he'd picked up on the way home and which clearly delighted Spencer. It was the Disney film *Cars*, which he'd already seen at the cinema, and couldn't wait to sit down with us and see again.

I went to bed happy that night, thinking that we might be making progress. I even let myself believe, given how badly the day had started, that the old Casey magic was beginning to work its spell. Which just goes to show that the adage holds true. Pride always comes before a fall.

However, it would be the following evening before I could see that. Like Wednesday, Thursday seemed to be a day full of positives. Spencer trotted into school happily – no break for the border – and when I picked him up, once again he was smiling. And he continued to smile until he'd finished his tea, upon which he told me that he wanted to play out.

'You can't, I'm afraid,' I said. 'You're still grounded, remember?'

'But I have to,' he whined. 'I told Connor I would.'

'Connor? Who's Connor?' I said. I didn't know the name.

'He lives up the road,' he said. 'He's my age. We speak out of our windows.'

'Out of your windows?' I asked, baffled. 'What d'you mean, speak out of your windows?'

'He's only two doors up,' he explained, as though any idiot would know that. 'We lean out of our bedroom windows and we chat. Please, Casey,' he pleaded, 'just for half an hour? I told him …'

'No, Spencer, you can't,' I said. 'And I don't want you leaning out of your bedroom window either. It's a skylight and it's dangerous to be leaning out of it.'

'But I said I'd call for him.'

'Well, you shouldn't have. You knew you were grounded. Rules are rules. You'll have to wait till Saturday – points permitting, you can call for him then.'

He acted so quickly right then that I was almost too late. One minute he was sitting there, looking all dejected, and the next he was out of the kitchen and in the hallway like an Exocet missile, only thwarted from escaping by our Yale lock. 'Spencer,' I snapped, 'what on earth do you think you're doing?'

He dropped his hands, defeated, and glared at me defiantly. 'You can't keep me in,' he yelled. 'I'm eight years old. Not a kid.'

If his sentiment about what age a 'kid' was sounded amusing, his defiance was definitely not. I stepped past him, turned the mortice-lock key below, and then removed it, while he pouted his disapproval before stomping into the living room. Here he turned. 'You can't keep it locked for ever,' he said to me. 'I'll be off as soon as you forget. Stupid idiot!'

Out in the kitchen, preparing fish and vegetables for tea, I felt cross with myself. I felt uncharacteristically wound up – and by a little boy of eight! I was also beginning to realise that all the improbable-sounding warnings this child had come with were little by little beginning to come true. I put the fish in the oven to cook and washed my hands. As Spencer was in the living room, watching TV now, perhaps I should go into the conservatory and call his social worker.

But it seemed Glenn had a slightly different take on things where Spencer was concerned. 'It sounds worse than it is,' he soothed, after I'd outlined the incident in school, his teacher's comments and the fact that he'd just tried to abscond from the house. 'I mean, I do know he's only eight, but he's not stupid. According to his parents he spends the majority of his days out on the streets – always has – and he can obviously take care of himself.'

I almost spluttered. 'So you're saying we should just leave him to run wild?'

'No, of course not,' he said. 'He obviously needs boundaries. It's boundaries that have been lacking in his life, clearly. All I'm saying is that if he does run you shouldn't worry unduly. He knows how to look after himself, and he always comes back. Just as soon as he gets cold or hungry.'

This seemed to beggar belief. This man was clearly not a parent. 'It's all very well you telling me he can look after himself, Glenn, but Spencer is our responsibility. I need to know that we can keep him safe. It's our professional responsibility to be sure we can protect him, and, frankly, him running around the streets unsupervised does not constitute a part of that. From what you say, we're going to have to start locking ourselves in.'

'I know,' he soothed again. 'I know that. And you're doing great. And if you have to keep the house locked to feel secure, then, obviously, so be it. I'm just trying to reassure you that he's not a typical eight-year-old. So if he *does* go missing, chances are he won't come to any harm.'

I finished the call feeling not more but even less reassured, Spencer's 'trendy' social worker obviously seeing things so differently to how I did. It wasn't even about what harm might befall him if he managed to run away. From what Glenn had said, that was the least of my worries. It was much more about the principle of what foster care was meant to be. How could I possibly create an environment of 'trust, mutual respect and comfort' when I had to behave like a prison guard? Not much of any of those three in that, was there?

I gave Mike a quick debrief when he arrived home from work, not least because I had to unlock the front door to let him in. We decided against him having a further disciplinary chat with Spencer tonight. Better to enjoy tea and keep the atmosphere light in the hopes that he'd feel a little less like doing his Houdini thing. And tea went well, with Spencer chatting animatedly about his paintings, and telling Mike how much he liked drawing in his sketch book. Even his hopes of perhaps becoming an artist one day.

'Would you like to see it?' Spencer asked him. 'I could go and get it now.'

'After tea,' Mike said. 'Then we can sit down and go through it properly. I'd enjoy that.'

Some hope, as it turned out.

Tea was over in double quick time, Spencer shovelling food in as if his life depended on it, and me all the while feeling pleased, at least on that front. Here was a child who would willingly eat fish and vegetables. And just as Mike was filling me in about an order from work, Spencer, his plate cleared, declared himself finished. 'Shall I go and get my sketch book now, Mike?' he wanted to know.

'Go on then,' chuckled Mike. 'You're obviously dying for me to see it. Off you go. I'll be done here by the time you're back down.'

Spencer ran off happily, and Mike continued with his story. Seconds later, however, he stopped abruptly. We had both heard the front door slamming shut.

At first I couldn't fathom it. The door had been double locked. I had the key. Then Mike groaned. 'Shit! I went out to the car, didn't I?' he realised. 'To get those papers. And left the key on the side in the kitchen … oh, shit!'

All that acting. All that desperate need to show Mike his sketch book. I felt the biggest fool, suddenly, on the planet. Spencer had been right in what he'd said to me. I *had* been a stupid idiot.

We ran to the door, down that path, onto the street. Spencer was nowhere to be seen.

# Chapter 6

What credulous fools we were, I couldn't help thinking, as we ran back to the house and Mike pulled his boots on.

'Should I phone someone, do you think?' I asked anxiously. I could already feel panic rising inside me. It was all very well Glenn telling me not to worry about Spencer, but this was an eight-year-old, and we were responsible for him.

Mike shook his head. 'Give me a chance to have a quick scout around first.' He headed back down the path, then stopped and turned around. 'Actually, do you think I should take the car instead?'

'No!' I couldn't help snapping. 'Just go! If you take the car you might miss him down an alley. Just hurry, will you? He could be miles away by now.'

Mike jogged off then, and I went back to keep an eye out from behind the window. It was only early autumn but there was a real nip in the air. And Spencer, as far as I knew, was only in pyjamas and slippers. Unless he'd whipped them off while up 'getting his sketch book for Mike'. God, I felt such a fool. I could only hope Mike found him before I had to ring the police and report him missing, and spare us a whole round of form filling and interventions and, worst of all, the admission that we'd failed.

It was a full half hour, the minutes inching onwards painfully slowly, before Mike returned. Unhappily, however, he was alone.

'Call the EDT, Casey,' he said. 'I've looked everywhere I can think of, but if he's hiding it's pointless. He won't show himself until he's ready to be found, will he?'

The EDT – or Emergency Duty Team – are a 24-hour on-call service, dedicated to social services. They are the first port of call in situations like this. They would provide us with back-up and advice and, most importantly, log the incident so that there was a permanent record on file of what had happened – something that was particularly important in cases of violence or harm, or a child reporting something untrue. I ran to the locked cabinet where I kept my fostering log book and Spencer's details, knowing from experience that they would ask me endless questions. It made sense to have the answers on hand.

Some minutes passed before the call with the EDT came to an end. They'd wanted a physical description, obviously, plus Spencer's home address. They also wanted any information I could give them about other people and addresses that might potentially help them track him down. That done, they then told me to call the police, so the whole process had to be repeated again.

'So what did they say?' Mike asked as I put the phone down for the second time. He passed me a mug of coffee.

'Thanks, love. That they're sending someone to us now, plus it'll have gone out to the patrol officers. With any luck, there'll be some looking for him right now.'

Mike shook his head. 'Little tyke,' he said, taking up my former position at the window. 'I hope this isn't going to be a regular occurrence.'

I went and joined him. His jaw was set and his face was pale with worry. 'He'll be okay, love,' I said, sliding an arm around his waist. 'Like you said, he's probably hiding. He'll show himself eventually. He won't want to be out long in this cold. He's just trying to teach us a lesson, isn't he? That he can beat the system. Get one up on us …'

'Exactly!' he said with feeling. 'And where does that leave us? What leverage do we have to help change his behaviour if he has the means to flout the rules whenever he doesn't like them?'

'Plenty,' I said. 'If he wants to play hardball then so will we. We must. While he's still young enough to *have* his behaviour modified.'

'In theory,' said Mike, peering into the blackness.

It was another two hours before there was a knock on the front door. Two hours in which we'd done nothing productive bar drink more mugs of coffee and fail to find something to distract us. This wasn't one of our own kids, but it didn't matter: we were *in loco parentis*, and our charge – the child who social services had entrusted to our safekeeping – had run away, which wasn't a nice feeling. Didn't matter how much we'd be reassured that there was nothing we could have done to stop him (which we would be) – if something happened to that little boy I would never forgive myself.

We flew to the door together, to see a policeman-shaped shadow behind the glass, and, to my immense relief, an eight-year-old-boy shape as well.

'Spencer!' I cried out as soon as I saw him. He was indeed in just his pyjamas and slippers. 'Oh, Spencer. God, you must be freezing! Come on, come in.'

Spencer's expression was forlorn, and the policeman looked stern. I got the impression that a dressing down had already been delivered. The first one, anyway. It wasn't going to be the last. But for the moment all I cared about was that he was back safely with us. Even though, as it turned out, it was by chance.

'I was on my way here to take your statement,' the policeman explained as I herded everyone into the warmth of the living room, 'when I saw this young man sitting on a wall at the top of your street.'

I saw Mike's jaw drop. 'You'd been sitting there all this time?' he asked Spencer. 'But I –'

'He was in a wheelie bin,' the policeman said, 'two doors up from here, hiding out. Till he got too cold. Been sitting there for, what, half an hour?'

Spencer mumbled confirmation.

'But why didn't you just come home, lad?' Mike asked. Spencer simply hung his head.

'A hot drink,' I said. 'That's what you need. Constable? Spencer?'

Now Spencer did look up, though he couldn't quite look me in the eye. 'Yes, please,' he said meekly. 'An' I'm sorry,' he proffered also.

I nodded, but stopped myself from saying 'That's okay', because it wasn't. He needed to know that actions had consequences, that they couldn't be cancelled out just by trotting out apologies. They had their place, of course, but they needed to be accompanied by actions. This child must not see me and Mike as soft touches.

The policeman declined a drink, saying that things wouldn't take too long now, and by the time I'd made Spencer's, Mike was showing him out. No need for lengthy statements when the incident's already over, after all.

'Come on, you,' I said to Spencer, after I'd been into the hall and thanked the constable. 'Into the kitchen for this hot chocolate. I've made you some toast as well.'

He followed me in and sat up at the table where I directed, then wound his fingers around his special mug.

'Can I still go out on Saturday?' he asked quietly, after taking a sip from it.

I looked at him, amazed. Boy, did we have a way to go. 'I'm sorry, love, but no. Of course you can't, not after this. What you've done tonight will add at least a few more days to your grounding.' He looked as if I'd just told him the sky had fallen in. 'Spencer, love, you can't just do as you please, you know. The adults make the rules and you – as the child – have to accept that.'

'Casey's right, lad,' Mike agreed, coming into the kitchen to join us. 'Rules are there for a reason. Most of the time they are there to keep you safe.' He turned to me. 'Grab

Spencer's points sheet, will you, Casey? Then we can look at how he stands as far as today goes.'

I reached for the sheet and joined the two of them at the table, while Mike quietly went through the points and rewards with Spencer, urging him to work out how they balanced by himself.

'So I won't get any polite and respect points today, then?' he asked.

I shook my head. 'Obviously not.'

'An' I don't suppose I'll be getting my "bed on time" points either?' We all looked at the clock then. It was way past 9 p.m.

'Obviously not,' I said again. I pointed to the chart. 'So you see, you couldn't afford to buy "peer time" in any case. Even without being grounded. You won't have earned sufficient points.'

For some reason, this seemed to make Spencer a little happier. He smiled. 'So I can't afford it,' he said.

Mike nodded. 'Exactly.'

I watched Spencer's expression changing and suddenly got a sense of what was happening here. He didn't mind because he felt this was something *he* controlled. He couldn't go out, not because *we'd* grounded him, but because *he* hadn't earned sufficient points. This obviously made it feel acceptable. I smiled to myself. At last I had an inkling of what made this little boy tick.

He picked his toast up. 'Okay,' he said cheerfully.

The weekend came and went without further drama or abscondings, and Spencer spent much of it engaged in productive endeavours like painting pictures and building Lego models. And he was delightful to have around, being both polite and helpful. He helped Mike to wash his car, and also really seemed to enjoy gardening. He spent three hours with us out in the back garden on the Sunday, 'shutting it down' for the coming winter. And he seemed to delight, like any little boy, in getting plastered in mud, as he enthusiastically unearthed an assortment of bugs and spiders, as he helped pull up the last of the straggly weeds.

But the kids who came to us didn't do so because they were impeccable little angels, so it was perhaps silly of me to have been lulled into a false sense of security. But I clearly had, as I found out the following Tuesday. In fact, I was brought down to earth with quite a bang.

It was an ordinary sort of Tuesday, so after dropping Spencer off at school I'd decided that once I'd done a bit of housework I'd pop into town. I had to go to the bank, and I also thought I'd take the opportunity to nip into my favourite children's shop, which was nearby. I was just setting off there when a car pulled up outside. It was Kieron and Lauren, wanting to come and use my internet.

'We'll come back later,' they said, seeing as I was obviously going out.

'No, it's fine,' I said. It was good to see them any time, of course, and, what with Spencer coming, it felt like we'd not seen enough of them lately, so I didn't want to send them packing the very minute they arrived. Far from it. 'Come in,' I said. 'You can do what you want to do, and then make us all some lunch for when I'm back. And then we can all have a proper catch-up.'

Happily they agreed to my cheeky request, and I trotted off, my day already lifted.

It was Levi's third birthday in November, just a few weeks away now, and my main aim while I was out was to pick him up some presents, so after I'd done my banking I had a lovely half hour choosing the sort of gorgeous little clothes for him – funky jeans and tiny chinos – that Riley wouldn't dream of splurging so extravagantly on herself. I wouldn't myself normally, but I was actually feeling a bit flush at the moment, having recently kicked my longstanding smoking habit, with the little ones being my main motivation.

With that in mind, I also popped into the chemist's and picked up some more herbal cigarettes; they were pretty foul but so far I'd managed to stay on board the wagon, so it was in a jaunty mood that I finally arrived home.

But it seemed Kieron and Lauren's was less so.

'Get the kettle on!' I shouted as I came in through the front door, only to have Lauren pop her head out from around the kitchen door frame, her index finger held against her lips.

'What's wrong?' I asked.

'Kieron's on the phone to school,' she whispered.

'To what school?' I asked, confused.

'To Spencer's school,' she explained, as I followed her into the living room, where Kieron was just now hanging up. His face was a picture of anguish.

'What's wrong, love?' I asked, fearing something dreadful had happened. Had Spencer run away again? Had some harm come to him? What?

Kieron shook his head sadly. 'You know your chain?' he started. 'Your one with the gold musical note, that Dad bought you?' I nodded. 'Well, they called to say Spencer's teacher has just found it in his tray – his tray at school. And seven pounds, as well.' He looked vexed now. 'Mum, where would he get seven pounds from?'

'My chain?' I parroted back at him, as I began to take it in.

Now Kieron's expression changed. 'Mum, it's not rocket science. He's obviously *stolen* it from you, hasn't he? *And* the money. He must have decided to start hiding the things he steals there instead. They're going to give them back to you when you go and collect him. Mum,' he persisted, clearly upset, 'why is he *doing* this?'

'I don't know, love,' I said, putting my shopping bags down finally. 'Because he can, I suppose. Because he just can't help himself. Because he's troubled. There's always a reason, deep down.'

'No, Mum,' Kieron said, 'there is no reason to steal. None at all. It's just horrible. Why does he *do* it?'

There was no answer I could give him that he could accept, and that was that. I felt for my son and understood how hard he found all this. He was a grown man now but, with his Asperger's, there was so much that still confused him. As well as hating change – which had always distressed him, since he was tiny – he found it genuinely emotionally difficult to process 'bad' and aberrant behaviours. Which our foster kids, unfortunately, tended to display in spade loads.

I saw Lauren slip her hand into his and squeeze it to reassure him. I worried about Kieron constantly – what mother wouldn't? – but his girlfriend was a godsend. I wasn't really religious but it seemed some deity must have had a hand in bringing someone to us who was so uniquely capable of understanding and coping with all the idiosyncrasies that made Kieron Kieron.

And he'd blossomed so much since they'd been together. They'd met at college and since then he'd really found himself a focus. Though he loved music and was still a keen amateur DJ, he'd now taken a part-time job in the café my sister owned, supporting himself while he trained for his chosen career as a youth worker. He'd really thrown himself into this, and was now shadowing a senior youth worker, and was also volunteering at a local youth club, where he was currently starting up a football team.

But seeing him now, I really worried about his choice of career. I had spent a long time pointing out to him that some of the children he'd come across in work would have problems, some as severe as the children we fostered, and he kept repeating that he was just fine with that. But he obviously wasn't. I could see that so clearly. Spencer's stealing had really upset him, and I hated to think he was embarking on work that had the capacity to make him so distressed.

'Love, don't worry,' I said now. 'I will deal with it. What you need to get your head around is that Spencer's lacked rules all his life. He's never had boundaries, which is why he doesn't understand them. But trust me, love, by the time he leaves us he'll be a completely different child.'

Kieron, I could see, was now relaxing a little. 'I hope so,' he said, 'because I can't be doing with stealing, Mum. Mucking about's one thing. But stealing's so *bad*.'

'Stop worrying,' Lauren said, putting her arm around him now. 'You know your mum – she'll soon lick him into shape, just like she always does. By the time she's done with him, you wait, he'll be a proper little angel.'

'He's more like a little devil at the moment,' Kieron huffed. 'An Oliver Twist.'

I shook my head. 'You mean Artful Dodger, don't you? I already thought that.'

'Well, whatever,' said Lauren. 'But *not* for much longer.'

I laughed with them, of course, but I wasn't sure I shared Lauren's confidence. I mentally rolled my sleeves up. I'd just have to hope she was right.

# Chapter 7

I continued fretting about Kieron all the way to school. I knew I shouldn't over-dramatise, but his reaction had unsettled me. His upset on hearing about Spencer's latest antics had been a bit over the top, even for him. Much as I didn't want to interfere or put him off, I sensed he had too much on his plate. What with managing his part-time job, and the youth-worker training, not to mention his determination to run this football team of his, I wondered if he was in danger of becoming overloaded. I really must, I told myself, as I waited for the school's electronic gates to open, make some space to spend a little bit more time with him and Lauren. And that went for Riley and David as well, up to their eyes in work and looking after their little family. I'd been much too preoccupied since Spencer had arrived, and needed to focus my energies a little more on my own family.

Mr Gorman and his little charge were walking down the corridor, coincidentally, just as I arrived in reception. 'Ah,' said Mr Gorman, 'I gather your son's told you about our, erm, news?'

I nodded and looked at Spencer. 'Well,' I said, 'what's all this about, then?'

Spencer's expression was defiant. 'I never took 'em, Casey,' he said. 'I just found 'em in my bag when I looked in it. But they won't believe me. They never do, this lot.'

'Excuse me, young man, less of that talk,' Mr Gorman said. He handed me an envelope. 'It's all in there,' he said. 'The necklace, plus the seven pounds in cash. What can I say? I suppose it's best if I leave things with you now?'

'Yeah,' Spencer moaned. 'So that means I get kept in again. Like I'm a pet, or something. I'm sick of this. No one *ever* believes me!'

He was still raging to himself as I steered him to the car, though once strapped into it he evidently decided it was pointless. His only words in response to my questioning were to insist again that he'd done nothing wrong.

Which was fine. It left my mind free to wander back to my own son. By the time I was home I had made up my mind. Sending Spencer to his room to get changed out of his uniform, I took my phone into the conservatory, along with one of my herbal cigarettes, and dialled John Fulshaw's number.

'Hi, Casey,' he answered cheerfully. 'How are things going, or shouldn't I ask?'

'No, you shouldn't,' I answered, 'but since you have, I shall tell you.' I then spent ten minutes recounting all Spencer's latest misdemeanours, up to and including the latest pilfering. 'Anyway,' I concluded, 'what I was ringing to ask was if it would be possible to arrange some respite care for the coming weekend. Just Friday, after school, round to the Monday would be great. I know we haven't had him long yet, but ...'

'Casey, slow down, and stop worrying. There's no need to justify yourself, you know that. I know he's been extremely challenging. God, it might not have been long, but he's certainly kept you busy. It's no wonder at all that you feel you need a break.'

'It's not so much me,' I said. God knew, I'd dealt with challenging children and then some over the years. 'It's the family, really. I feel they need more of a piece of me right now. Kieron's got this new job, which is really stressing him out, and, well, as you know, Riley's got a new baby and everything. It's all just been a bit full on, really, just recently ...' I was rambling on a bit, but I sensed that was no bad thing anyway. It was necessary for John to know how much I needed this. And he clearly did.

'Consider it done,' he reassured me. 'Well, as good as. I'll have to speak to Spencer's social worker, but I do have a couple who might do it. They're at a loose end right now, so if they don't have any plans ...'

I uttered a silent thank you as I hung up the phone. I was confident John would come through with his promise. And if it couldn't be this weekend, I was sure it would be the next one, which would be fine. It was just really important that Mike and I spend time with our children and grand-children without Spencer – not to mention various belong-ings' whereabouts – being the number one topic of conversation.

I'd just gone back into the kitchen when the boy himself trotted down, looking like butter wouldn't melt in his mouth, and asked if it was okay to watch TV. It irked me slightly to say yes, given his latest misdemeanour, but this was using up points he'd already earned yesterday, so I had no choice: the system was the system. Initially it had felt like a flaw in the programme, but actually it wasn't. It was one of its strengths. The whole point was that it put the child in control. Instead of heat-of-the-moment punishments, quickly administered, soon forgotten, the system of earning points allowed space to reflect. When a punishment came later – as would be the case with today's pilfering – the child had the result of their actions better reinforced. As they sat bored without their privileges, as Spencer would do tomorrow, they could better appreciate the wisdom of thinking before acting, before potentially spoiling yet another day.

Having installed him in the living room I got on with pulling out the ingredients for tea, but it was only minutes later when the phone rang. It was John again.

'Right,' he said. 'Sorted. Pack him a bag for this weekend. It's a Mr and Mrs Pemberton and they're happy to take him straight after school. Glenn will collect him and deposit him, and all you have to do is go to pick him up late on Sunday, if that'll work for you?'

'It'll more than work, John. That's brilliant. Thanks so much for doing this. So I send him to school Friday packed and ready then, am I right?'

It seemed I was. John went on to explain the directions, and also instructed me to give them a ring, before Friday,

71

just to fill them in about Spencer's routines. The Pembertons lived on a farm, an hour's drive away. A rural idyll, I thought. Perfect. I mentally began planning our weekend. Then I picked the phone up again and dialled Mike's work number, keen to tell him the good news and also to prepare him. We could then tell Spencer together, over tea.

Respite care is a basic part of fostering, understandably. When your job is so full-on – as it often was, particularly with our kind of fostering – it's important that there's a system in place that gives the carers a break if they need one. Up to now, however, it hadn't been something I'd felt we'd needed. So far, we'd hardly ever made use of it.

So I didn't feel too bad as we sat down to eat our cottage pie. We'd have a couple of days off, to spend with family, and Spencer would have a small adventure. And on a farm, too, which would be such fun for him. John had told me the Pembertons were a really nice couple, who'd make Spencer's stay with them great. And that's how I billed it when I told him.

'Guess what, Spencer?' I said to him, as I picked up my cutlery. 'You're going on a bit of an adventure this weekend.'

Spencer had started scooping peas up with his fork. Now he stopped and eyed me suspiciously. 'What, me?' he said. 'Even after I've been bad and nicked that stuff?'

Ah, an admission at last. Probably the only one I'd get. I mentally filed it, for my journal. 'Yes, you,' I said brightly. 'Though, to be truthful, it's also a little break for Mike and me as well.'

'What, you're coming too?' he asked.

I shook my head. 'No, it's just you. We'll be staying here.'

His expression clouded. 'Are you sending me away?'

He looked upset now, and I glanced at Mike, hoping he'd reassure him. 'No, we're not sending you away, Spencer. You're just off on a little holiday. Glenn's going to pick you up after school on Friday, and take you to stay on a farm for the weekend. Won't that be fun? Like a little adventure. While Casey and I have a rest. Then we'll come and get you and bring you home again on Sunday night.'

Spencer digested this news along with a couple more forkfuls of peas. He seemed to like eating this way. Plough through the veg first: get them out of the way. Then he looked up at Mike again. 'Like with pigs and all that?'

'I imagine so. And maybe other animals, too. And lots of fresh air.'

'Okay,' he said, nodding. Then he put his head down and tucked into the rest of his tea. So far so good, I decided, so roll on the weekend. And the week then really did seem to fly by. I was in good spirits, knowing I'd have a clear weekend with the family, and booked a table for us all at one of our favourite restaurants, a steak house the kids had loved since they were young. With any luck, David's mum would babysit for a couple of hours, too, so we could all relax and enjoy a few drinks.

Spencer too seemed in a cheerful, obliging mood. When I picked him up from school on Thursday he came out brandishing a huge picture. 'For Mr and Mrs Pemberton, this is,' he told me proudly. 'Look, see, this is a tractor, cos

they've got them on farms, and these are the chickens …
do foxes kill chickens, Casey?'

'Um, yes they do, Spencer. Sometimes …'

'I knew that!' His little face was suddenly animated by
indignation. 'But Mr Gorman said they didn't and that I
couldn't paint dead chickens. I wished I *had* of …'

I shook my head in wonder at this strange little lad.
'Perhaps Mr Gorman was right, love,' I said. 'Perhaps he
just meant that the picture would look nicer for the
Pembertons if it didn't have any dead chickens in it.'

'Aww, yes, I s'pose …' he agreed, smiling his angelic
smile at me. 'Can I take my art things to the farm, do you
think? Then I can paint the real chickens, can't I?'

'Which won't be dead, we hope, eh?' I agreed,
laughing.

The next morning, however, his mood was more sombre,
and I was stunned, as I went to leave him at the school
reception, when he suddenly wrapped his arms around me,
completely without warning. It was the first time he'd done
something so spontaneous and affectionate. 'I'll miss you,
Casey,' he said, his voice muffled as his face was pressed so
close against me. 'I've left Fluffy Cow outside your
bedroom door.'

'Have you? Didn't you want to take him?'

I felt him shake his head. 'I want you to look after him
while I'm away. Can he sleep in your bed till I come back?'
I was really shocked, and found a lump begin to form in my
throat. Then I reminded myself this was two days on a
farm, not a Second World War evacuation, for heaven's

sake. 'Of, course,' I said. 'Of course he can, and, listen, you mustn't worry. You just have a lovely time there, okay?' I bent down then and kissed the top of his head, and, seemingly satisfied, he let me go and backed away down the corridor, waving before turning to head off to his classroom. I watched him go. From the back he looked such a sorry sight, bowed slightly under the weight of his enormous bulging rucksack. He turned again, at the end, to wave once more.

What a funny little thing he was, I reflected as I drove home. What sort of home life had made him what he was – so street-wise and swaggering, so accomplished in the ways of thieving, yet so vulnerable and so young for his age in other ways. I would find out, no doubt – well, get some idea about it, eventually. For now, though, I switched gear – this was a weekend for family. Out of sight, I decided, out of mind for a bit. He'd probably do likewise, and have a ball.

And we did have a wonderful weekend. Mike and I spent the Friday night with a takeaway and a couple of movies, and after a blissfully relaxed day with Riley and the babies, our Saturday-night family meal was just wonderful. It was so nice to just sit and laugh and swap anecdotes and reminisce, and also to reassure myself that Kieron seemed just fine. Perhaps I worried unduly. He seemed both relaxed and happy, regaling us with stories about his travels – and travails – with his youth worker, and the ongoing challenge of getting his footie team up to scratch.

Come Sunday morning, I even woke up with a slight hangover, something I'd not 'enjoyed' for quite a while.

But for all the headache – soon dispatched with a couple of ibuprofen – I also felt happy and recharged. 'Ready for action again?' I asked Mike, who seemed similarly chilled.

'Oh, if we must,' he joked, winking.

And it seemed we would need to be, and sooner than we'd thought. I'd planned on doing a big family roast late afternoon, but it seemed that my plans were about to change. My mobile phone rang while I was plating up some scrambled eggs and bacon. Mike rummaged in my handbag and pulled it out for me.

I read the display as he passed it to me. John Fulshaw. What did *he* want? It was Sunday. Then it hit me. John phoning was likely to only mean one thing …

'It's Spencer,' he said, confirming it, as I pressed the answer button. 'I'm so, so sorry to ruin what's left of your weekend, but you're going to need to go and pick him up from the Pembertons.'

'Oh, no,' I said, feeling my *joie de vivre* drain away. 'What's wrong? What's happened?'

'What *hasn't* is more about the size of it, apparently. He's caused havoc, I'm told, and they really want him gone.'

'Shit! But what's he done? I can't believe this …'

'I know. From what I can gather, he decided to try and drive their tractor. Unsupervised. He's knocked down a wall, or so I'm told, and …'

'Is he hurt?'

'Oh, no. *He's* not. But some of the animals are …'

'Did he run them down? Oh, my lord!'

'No, not at all. That's completely separate, they tell me. He's been terrorising the animals all weekend, apparently.

Scaring the chickens, worrying sheep – whatever worrying sheep means … Even kicking one. One that was already injured, Glenn tells me, and –'

'Okay, John. I get the gist. We'll get dressed and be on our way.'

'So?' asked Mike, brows raised, having heard my side of the conversation.

'So, bye-bye happy weekend,' I said miserably.

# Chapter 8

It was almost an hour before Mike and I arrived at the farm, and as we pulled into the entrance I braced myself for a frosty reception. She'd seemed really nice, Mrs Pemberton, when I'd spoken to her on the phone on the Friday, and I felt guilty that, while I'd warned her about Spencer's light-fingered antics and tendency to run off, at no point had I said – because it had never occurred to me in a million years – that he'd cause the sort of havoc he apparently had.

'I bet they're not too happy with us,' I told Mike as he parked the car.

'They'll be fine,' he consoled me. 'It's hardly our fault, love, is it? And anyway, they're foster carers too, so it's not like they're not used to it. They'll understand. You'll see.'

The farm was large, and clearly a working one. As we walked from the car we could see pigs, cows and sheep dotted in the patchwork of surrounding fields. The house itself was huge – it looked more like a mansion than a farmhouse. What a wonderful place for any foster child to end up. I thought back to little Olivia, one of the pair of siblings we'd last fostered. She'd gone to a family who lived on a farm and I knew she'd already settled really well there. Spencer, however, clearly hadn't embraced the outdoor life. I gritted my teeth as Mike reached to press the doorbell.

It was Mr Pemberton who answered, and though he smiled warmly enough the strain showed in his face. 'Quite a little handful you've got there, haven't you?' he said in hushed tones as he showed us in. 'He's in there,' he said, nodding his head towards a half-open door into a living room. 'With my wife, Catherine. Go on. Go right in.'

We walked into the room Mr Pemberton indicated to see Spencer sitting in a rocking chair, being spoken to by Mrs Pemberton, in what appeared to be firm but quite reasonable terms. But when he saw me, you'd be forgiven for thinking otherwise. He jumped from the chair so dramatically, he nearly upended it in the process, and flew towards me with tears streaming down both his cheeks. Once he got to me he launched himself at me, sobbing. 'Oh Casey, oh Mike!' he wailed. 'Please take me home to yours. It's rubbish here. I promise I'll never be bad again, honest. Honestly – I swear on me mother's life!'

'Spencer, love, come on,' I soothed, rather startled at his distress. I felt torn between comforting him – in front of the rather bemused-looking couple – and taking him to task about all the things he'd done. Mrs Pemberton partic- ularly, however, didn't look too impressed at his histrionics, and I decided that rather than pick over the apparently

*Casey Watson*

lengthy list of misdemeanours, a 'least said soonest mended' policy might be the best one.

'I think we'll head straight off. Leave you in peace,' I said to the Pembertons, glancing at Mike for corroboration. He nodded. 'Give you a ring in the morning, if that's okay,' I added.

Spencer's sobbing at this comment grew to a wailing. 'Don't send me away again,' he pleaded, clearly concerned that this obviously wasn't the end of it. 'I'll be good from now on, Casey. Honestly I will!'

It was only a small gesture. But I saw Mrs Pemberton roll her eyes. We shuffled out. No point in prolonging the agony.

Spencer continued to cry all the way home. Every time we tried to discuss what had happened to him, he just dissolved into shoulder-racking sobs, pleading with us not to talk about it. Just kept promising over and over that if we didn't send him away again he'd be a good boy from now on. I felt bad. I clearly shouldn't have arranged the weekend respite. It had been too soon. It had also been just after the last incident, and he clearly saw it as some sort of punishment. Was that why he'd played up and done all those dreadful things? I could have kicked myself. Because now we had to deal with the fall-out.

'Look, Spencer,' I tried, as we got close to home, 'I know it's difficult, being reminded about things you did that aren't so nice, but we have to talk about it, love, otherwise it'll be like they never happened. But they did.' I turned around to where he was huddled in the back seat. 'Do you understand? You did wrong and you can't just expect it to go away.'

He buried his head in his hands, like a small child might do: If you can't see it, it no longer exists. 'Look, I don't know all the ins and outs, Spencer,' I went on, 'but what I do know is that you tried to drive a tractor – and could have really hurt yourself – and that you also did some very unkind things to the Pembertons' animals. Spencer, you're eight, quite old enough to know the difference between right and wrong. Look at me, Spencer. What on earth were you *thinking*?'

He lifted his head. 'That sheep was stupid!' he said. 'An' it was mean. It was going to bite me!'

I'd never seen a sheep bite someone unprovoked in my entire life and I said so. But it fell on deaf ears. 'I know it was,' he persisted.

'Spencer, the Pembertons told me it was *injured*. You shouldn't have been harassing the poor animal in the first place …'

'I hate farms!' he burst out – and, in cutting across me, confirming it. 'I hate farms and I hate the Pembertons. They're old and they're stupid. They wouldn't let me do *anything*!'

'Which is not a reason to take yourself off trying to drive tractors and being unkind to animals, is it? Well, *is* it?'

Spencer, without an answer to that, fell silent once again. No one spoke for the remainder of the journey home.

\* \* \*

Spencer was contrite and subdued for the rest of the day, and I hoped that he was starting to reflect on what he'd done. I felt sorry once again that I'd been so quick to send him off to respite, and wondered if it had undone what little good we'd achieved so far. Totting it up, it really didn't seem much. And after dropping Spencer at school the following morning, and calling Glenn, it seemed even less progress than I'd imagined. Glenn told me the Pembertons thought him an evil little boy, a cruel and vicious child who had no thought for anyone or anything but his own amusement. They'd said they certainly wouldn't be offering to do respite for him again, and had also, for good measure, told Glenn that, because of having him, they would no longer look after children in his age group.

I was a little piqued at this, feeling a small flare of loyalty for the little boy who'd come into our lives. As foster carers, couldn't they be a little more understanding? But then I reflected that Mike and I probably weren't the same as other carers, in that we'd actively chosen to take on kids like Spencer – the ones everyone else had given up on.

Yet Spencer was different again. If he'd come from the care system – from a children's home, or from a neglectful, at-risk sort of family – then his lack of boundaries and empathy would be par for the course. Spending a long time being passed around in care or coming from a chaotic or abusive home obviously took its toll on a child. Over time, and lacking those two vital ingredients – love and boundaries – they invariably developed challenging attitudes and behaviours – it would be strange if they didn't.

But Spencer didn't fit that mould at all. Yes, he'd spent a little time with a temporary carer, but, to all intents and purposes, he'd come to us straight from a family home. Which meant from a *family* – a mum and dad, bunch of siblings, all together, no previous history – that was unusual in the very fact that, superficially at least, it *did* have those ingredients. So how come he seemed so very damaged? I pondered this aloud to Glenn, who agreed.

'Well, you might get more of an inkling next weekend, as it happens,' he said.

'Oh, really?' I said. 'How come?'

'Well, assuming it's okay with you, and that you don't have a prior engagement that precludes it, you'll be taking Spencer for his first home-contact visit then. I was due to be calling you to confirm it. You beat me to it.'

Hearing this was really good news, and it cheered me up no end. Perhaps seeing his family again might be just the thing Spencer needed. Though it had not escaped my notice that it had been Spencer himself who'd asked to go into care, I felt surer than ever that this was not a real desire to escape them but a desperate cry for help, a way of saying, 'Notice me. Show me love. *Give* me boundaries!'

And it seemed that the parents had readily agreed to the visit, too, which wasn't always the case. Far from it. In fact, in my first experience of fostering, the opposite had been true. Justin's mother had a long history of picking up and dumping her child, seemingly on a whim. In reality, it matched both her drug use and her love life; she'd have him home and then tire of him, then have him back … it went on for years, and the most heartbreaking thing was that poor Justin never gave up hope that the next time he went home it would be for ever. Of course, it never was and for me it was a depressing reminder that, in the main, children become 'bad' because they are treated badly. I so hoped Spencer's family would serve him better.

So this news was very definitely a positive. And who knew? Perhaps they'd feel able to have him home sooner rather than later. I couldn't wait to meet them and get some sort of handle on them.

It seemed Spencer felt the same. When I picked him up from school that afternoon and told him about the upcoming home visit, he couldn't have been more excited. Indeed, it was almost as if he'd completely forgotten that it was him who had asked to be put into care. He spoke lovingly about his siblings and, as the week went on, really opened up to us, telling Mike and me all sorts of funny stories about antics they got up to together. There was one point, though, where I got that familiar Casey prickle – a sense of how things under the surface were far from okay. It was when I asked him – just as something that came up in conversation – who he looked most like, his mum or his dad. Unusually, Spencer had come without photos. The kids we took on came from lots of different backgrounds, but all so far, bar the siblings we'd just said goodbye to, had some sort of cache of photos and souvenirs. But Spencer had come with nothing – lots of clothes, but no mementoes. So I had no idea what any of his family looked like. And the question seemed to stop him in his tracks. He looked at me strangely before answering, 'My mum.'

'She's got your lovely coppery hair, too, has she?' I answered, still trying to read him as I ruffled his.

'I look like my mum,' he repeated. 'That's what my dad says. An' I'm like her, too. That's what he says. "You're *just* like your mother."'

It was strange, the way he said this. Not proudly, at all. Indeed, I was aware of a real edge in his voice now. But then he abruptly changed the subject, and I decided I wouldn't push it. I had evidently touched a raw nerve.

Apart from that one slightly bizarre moment, however, Spencer's excitement continued growing. So much so that, come Saturday morning, he was like a bottle of pop. 'Oh, Casey,' he said, as he punched his arms into his jacket sleeves, 'bet they can't wait to see me. What do you think? D'you think they will be dying to see me? I expect they'll be so sad I've been gone from home so long!' He laughed. 'I bet you *any* money they'll ask me to come home again. I'm gonna take Fluffy Cow, I think. Yeah, that's what I'll do. Won't be a minute. I gotta take him because Harvey really loves him.' With which he belted up the stairs, two at a time, to fetch him.

By now I was beginning to feel the first stirrings of unease. With such high expectations I knew we were heading for a fall. I stepped outside, where Mike was clearing all the rubbish from inside the car. Though I was borderline obsessive about keeping my house like a show home, I didn't attach the same importance to the interior of the family runaround, and today's haul was typical: crisp wrappers, empty soft-drinks bottles, stray carrier bags, baby toys.

'Do you think we should prepare him?' I asked Mike, as he stretched across to clear the back footwell. 'I mean, just a bit of a reality check about things? I just feel that if we don't he's going to be so bitterly disappointed …'

Mike backed out, bearing a full carrier of rubbish, which he passed to me with an accompanying eye-roll. 'Not sure you can, love,' he said thoughtfully. 'Not without bursting his balloon, so to speak. And it's probably pointless. In his current state I doubt he'd take it in anyway.'

At which point Spencer burst from the house, grinning widely, with Fluffy Cow mouthing his excitement for him, while he jumped up and down on the spot.

'Are we going now?' the glove puppet wanted to know. Mike was right. Best to just see what happened.

In the end, I did manage to say something which I hoped would temper Spencer's expectations. We spent most of the journey (at my suggestion, so I could hardly complain) listening once again to Spencer's favourite, the Chipmunks. And a good way into it – it would be a three-hour round trip – he exclaimed that the track that had just started playing was one that he and his mum liked to sing along to together. 'I could take it with me,' he said. 'Could I do that, d'you think, Casey? My mum would love that. We could play it. Would that be okay? Bet she'll have missed that. Y'know. Playing with me an' that.'

I turned around in my seat. 'That would be fine, love,' I said. 'And you're right. I bet she *has* missed you. Lots.'

'An' she might want me home, you know. Like now. Like straight away.'

I was about to answer, when he spoke again. 'Cos I'm a changed kid, aren't I, Casey? I mean, *anyone* can see that.'

I smiled and nodded. 'In *lots* of ways,' I agreed. 'Yes, you are. You're doing brilliantly. Though,' I paused, 'there's still a plan we have to work to – you know, with social services. Which I think we *do* have to stick to. For the time being, anyway. But you know, if this visit goes well, then the next step will be that you'll be able to have overnight visits, and then your mum – *and* your dad – will be able to see just how well you're doing, won't they?'

Once again, at the mention of Spencer's dad I noticed this reaction. I couldn't put my finger on what the reaction was, but it was there.

But it was soon gone. 'Oh, we're nearly here!' he suddenly exclaimed, glancing out of the car window. 'Look, Fluffy Cow! We're nearly home.'

I glanced out as well. The family lived on a small estate that I'd been told was owned by a housing association, as was our own home. It seemed a perfectly nice, perfectly respectable area, and as Spencer pointed out all the places where he played with his friends I wondered again at how this boy had turned out to be so challenging; so bad that another foster carer called him 'evil'.

'An' here's the woods,' he said, pointing to a fuzz of tree-tops behind the houses. 'We make dens there, an' there's a stream there. We play lots there in the summer. One time, we even camped out. It was wicked.'

At just eight, this did surprise me. Had I allowed my children to play unsupervised in such places so young? And overnight? But I knew better than to interrupt. You learned so much more by listening. And within seconds we were outside his house anyway, and he was busily gathering up his bits and bobs.

'Home, Fluffy Cow!' he chirruped, as he trotted in front of us, up the path, to where a woman who I presumed to be a grandmother was waiting in the open doorway.

'Hi, Mum,' Spencer said, however, shocking me. Though she was not so old as to completely stun me, seeing his mother did surprise me. She just looked so much older than I'd envisaged, with markedly greying hair and a weather-beaten complexion. She was painfully thin too, and looked worn out and drawn. No cuddles were exchanged either; she merely gave him a thin smile as he shot past her into the house.

She looked at Mike. 'What time are you coming back for him?' she asked. Mike looked at his watch. 'About four o'clock, I thought.' He glanced at me. I nodded.

'Hi, I'm Casey,' I said. 'Kerry, isn't it? Will four be okay for you?'

Her nod was almost imperceptible. 'See you at four, then,' she said, stepping back into her hallway.

Very odd, I thought, as we walked back down the front path. No ceremony, no small talk, very little in the way of anything. 'So, what d'you think, love?' I asked Mike as we climbed back into the car.

He put the key in the ignition. 'Either very rude or very nervous about meeting us is what I think. Not decided which yet, to be honest,' he finished as we drove off.

Although it was still only the end of September, we'd decided to use our time to do a little early Christmas shopping. We'd have a mooch around, a bit of lunch, and then maybe do a little more. I'd been looking forward to it, actually, once I'd found out where Spencer's family lived, as there was a huge shopping mall only a short drive away. But now I was preoccupied. What an odd ten minutes that had been. No hugs exchanged, no sign of warmth – perhaps these were things I should have expected. After all, Spencer was in care for a reason. But I'd been shocked by his mother. Shocked by how different she'd been to what I imagined.

'She just looks so much older than I expected,' I said to Mike, as we sped along. 'Mind you, with five kids to look after – and with one of them being Spencer – well, I guess that probably ages you, doesn't it? But whatever her age, she just looked so haggard, don't you think? Not at all what I expected. Do you think she might be ill?'

'No one's said that, have they?'

I shook my head. 'Not to my knowledge. And they don't look badly off or anything, do they? Except she looked, well, just so dishevelled. Which is a bit weird when you think of all that designer kit Spencer has …'

'Who knows what goes on, love, eh? I dare say we'll learn more as we go, though in the meantime …'

We'd just turned off the A road into the mall. 'Ooh, shops!' I cried with glee, mentally switching gears. I would put Spencer firmly out of my mind for a few hours.

\*   \*   \*

As always happens when you try to fit a quart into a pint pot, there weren't sufficient hours in the day to do everything I'd planned to, and it was nearer half past by the time we pulled back up outside the family home. So yet again I was braced for a frosty reception as Mike raised his hand to press the doorbell.

Spencer's mum, however, must have already seen or heard us. The door opened just as Mike's finger touched the buzzer, though this time she only opened it a fraction. Looking at her, I decided it wasn't rudeness we'd seen earlier, just a complete absence of social skills. She looked blankly at us both.

'He's gone,' she informed us.

'*What?*' I said. 'Gone where?'

Now she shrugged. 'I don't know,' she said, her voice becoming slightly more animated, as though my asking such a question was just plain stupid. And that my incredulous expression was too. 'He lasted half an hour and then he was off,' she explained.

Which was no use to anyone. 'But –' I began saying to her. *But what?* I thought grimly, with the image of yet another two-hour police search of all the neighbouring wheelie bins.

She looked at me with the same needled but slightly glazed expression, and as she exhaled in what was presumably exasperation at life generally, I got a powerful whiff of alcohol on her breath. 'We couldn't stop him,' she said defensively. 'If he says he's going, then he's going. What am I supposed to do? Pin him to the ground?'

Mike had smelled it too, I knew. 'I can't believe this,' he said irritably. 'Is your husband there, Kerry? Because I think I'd like to speak to him.'

Yes, I thought crossly. Me too.

# Chapter 9

It was almost as if Spencer's father had been hiding behind a doorway, listening. No sooner were the words out of Mike's mouth than he appeared in the hallway, a tall, fit-looking man, with arrestingly blue eyes. As he smiled I immediately registered how different he seemed to his wife. He looked younger, for a start. Smarter. Altogether less dishevelled. He smiled apologetically.

'Danny,' he said. 'Look, I'm so sorry about all this.' He proffered his hand. 'You must be Mike. It's good to meet you at last,' he added. 'Casey, hi.' He shook hands with both of us while his wife looked on blankly. 'Spencer's told us lots about you,' he continued. 'Well, in the short time he was here, that is ...'

He made a small gesture then – a slight roll of the eyes, aimed loosely in his wife's direction. It wasn't an irritable gesture, just one that seemed to say, 'Well, you can see how it is, can't you?'

'I'd hoped the lad would have come back of his own accord by now,' he went on, leaning out to scan the darkening street. 'But, well, as you can see …' He tailed off, now, and sighed heavily.

I suddenly felt dreadfully sorry for him. He was obviously distressed and trying to make up for his wife's rudeness. Which made me soften towards him. 'It's not your fault,' I said. 'If Spencer was determined to run off, then I imagine there wasn't very much you could do about it. We had a similar experience two weeks back, to be honest. In the end we had to call the police.'

Spencer's father looked panicked then, as if the suggestion suddenly made everything more serious.

'The police? Do you think we should ring them, then?'

Mike had already pulled out his mobile from his pocket. 'I'll call them now,' he said, turning to walk back down the front path, pressing numbers as he went.

I turned back to Spencer's father. 'Have you any idea of where he might have gone?'

Danny shook his head. 'He could be anywhere. He knows these streets like the back of his hand. Believe me, if he doesn't want to be found, he won't be.'

His wife, who had remained silent throughout, now spoke. 'I'm going to see to the baby,' she said tonelessly. 'There's nothing I can do out *here*, is there?'

She sloped off, then, without so much as a word in my direction and, once again, I got the impression she'd had quite a lot to drink. Her husband's expression seemed to confirm it. 'Look, I'm really sorry …' he began again.

'It's fine,' I said. 'Don't worry. We'll get this sorted out.'

'I can't thank you enough,' he said. 'Honestly. It's been so tough for my wife just lately, what with me working such horrendous hours at the hospital – I work at the local general – but you probably know that. And we're so short staffed, and, well, what with everything with Spencer … him being so, well, difficult … it just makes us feel so hopeless. You know, as parents. We feel so lucky that there are people like you and Mike around …'

He trailed off yet again, clearly upset. I sympathised. He seemed like a well-meaning man in a very bad place. I wondered if his wife's drinking was a root cause or just a symptom of something else. She was clearly troubled. Depressed? Or did she have mental-health problems? Hard to tell. It felt like there was a great deal more to know about this family. But as I'd suspected – and had now seen for myself – *something* was far from right. It was just a case of finding out what that something was.

Mike came back then. 'They've told us to head home,' he announced to both of us. 'Said they'll send a car out now and that they'll return him to us as soon as they pick him up.'

'Bet that's the last thing they could do with on a Saturday evening,' I answered. 'Having to drive an eight-year-old runaway an hour and a half home.'

I felt slightly bad as soon as the words were out – it felt so barbed a comment. It hadn't been meant that way, but that's what it had sounded like, I realised. As if I was pointing out that the Herringtons could now close their front door and get on with their evening, leaving the problem very squarely in *our* laps.

But if he thought that, Danny Herrington didn't react to it that way. 'I'm so sorry,' he said sincerely. '*Really*. To put you to all this trouble. Oh, and you'd better have his backpack.' He picked it up from the hall floor. From somewhere in the house I could hear small children giggling. A happy sound. A normal family sound. Which right now felt so wrong.

'Forget it, mate,' Mike said, taking it. 'It's our job. It's what we do. We'll give you a call when he's returned to us, just so you know all's well.'

'I'd appreciate that,' Spencer's dad answered. 'I really would.'

'Well, that was weird,' Mike observed once we were back in the car. The police had told us to call the EDT as well, which I'd do as soon as we were on the road home. 'Weirder than weird, didn't you think? You know, standing on their doorstep, organising the return of *their* child to *our* house. If they can find him, that is, the little bugger.'

But for all his words, I knew Mike thought the same thing as I did. *Poor* little bugger, having a mum so totally out of it that she didn't even seem to care that her eight-year-old boy had run off and could be absolutely anywhere. I tried to get inside her head – imagine myself in that situation with my own kids – and couldn't. I sighed. Pointless to try. In the scheme of things, compared with some of the mothers of kids we'd fostered, her probable inebriated form of neglect was comparatively benign. At least she wasn't torturing him or sexually abusing him.

As far as we knew, at any rate. 'I felt sorry for the dad,' I told Mike. 'He was obviously trying to protect her. Maybe he's had a bit of a job on trying to hold things together. You know, the way she is and everything.

'But surely they must have half-expected this to happen?' I went on. 'Surely *he* would have, at least? Given Spencer's history – well, you'd have thought they'd have locked the doors, wouldn't you? All feels a bit pathetic, you know? A bit insubstantial.'

'Maybe he'd been out when we arrived, and it happened before he got home, or something.'

'Good point.'

'Or just maybe they're not fit to parent him,' Mike finished. He laughed. 'It's been known, love. There'd be no need for the likes of us, otherwise, would there?'

'I suppose so,' I said, dialling EDT.

It would be a further two hours after getting home before we were reunited with our little Houdini, who was standing sheepishly on the doorstep, dwarfed by a big burly policeman.

'Spencer,' I said firmly. 'Where on earth have you *been*?'

The constable ran a hand over Spencer's hair. It was so silky it was like no one could ever resist it. 'Found him sauntering around his estate, didn't I, kiddo? I think he knows he's in bother, Mrs Watson, don't you, lad?'

Spencer looked up at me with huge eyes. He looked exhausted. I saw Fluffy Cow was clutched in his hand. 'I'm sorry, Casey. I just didn't know what time it was.' He stepped into the hall.

'Well, I guessed that,' I said, as we followed him into the kitchen. 'You were gone for hours. Didn't you realise how upset and worried we'd all be? Your mum and dad were going out of their minds.'

Spencer's expression was clear. This didn't impress him one bit. He even snorted before answering. 'No they weren't!' he said indignantly. 'They don't even care.' He flopped down on a kitchen chair and lay his arms on the table, then put his head down on them, as if to endorse this. The policeman patted him, while Mike reached for the kettle.

I pulled up another chair and sat beside him. 'Love, you can't keep *doing* this,' I said gently. 'It's dangerous. You're much too young to be out, especially with the nights getting so dark now. And of *course* people care, and that *includes* your mum and dad.'

Spencer lifted his head, then, and I could see his cheeks were wet. He rubbed at them crossly, as if not wanting the policeman to see them. 'No they don't! I was saying how I've been such a good lad – I had a picture in my pocket for my mum, and everything, but she didn't even look at it.' His voice cracked, and now he'd started really sobbing. 'She just said, "Later, Spencer. I've got to see to the others." Just like always.'

'Oh, love,' I said, pulling him towards me for a cuddle. 'I'm sure she didn't mean it to sound bad. She's just frazzled. She must be so busy … what with five kids to look after …'

'Four,' Spencer corrected, his voice angry. 'Only *four*.'

I didn't know what to say to that. I just had to let him cry. Cry it out while the policeman, who'd turned down the offer of a coffee, was shown out by Mike.

He came to sit with us too, then, while I sat and rocked Spencer. He cried for a good ten minutes, but, eventually, he was spent. He sniffed loudly, and wiped his face with the back of the hand that held his puppet.

'That's the way, mate,' said Mike. 'Dry your eyes. Feeling a bit better now that's out of you?'

Spencer nodded. 'I'm okay,' he said. 'Just a bit tired. Can I get my 'jamas on?'

'Of course,' I said, standing up. 'Then I'll get you some supper, shall I? You must be starving.'

Spencer too climbed down from the table. Then shook his head.

'No, I'm fine,' he said to both of us, looking suddenly much brighter. 'I'm full of scraps.'

'Scraps?' Mike asked.

'Yeah,' he said, grinning now, as if locking on to a happier memory. 'Scraps from the chippy. He's sound, the man there is. He always gives me free bags of scraps. With lots of vinegar. I always tell him Mum forgot to give me dinner, and he's like, "You're like the kid who cried wolf, you – I never know whether to believe you!" But then I wink and he winks and he gives me a bag of scraps.'

Artful Dodger? Oliver Twist? Combination of both? It didn't matter. All I knew was that our Spencer was one singular little boy. He had this weird capacity to turn his emotions on and off. One minute in bits, and for what seemed *very* good reasons. But the next? I watched him trot upstairs with Mike to get his pyjamas on. It was as if he no longer had a care in the world.

# Chapter 10

I couldn't work out if the two things were related, but after the disastrous home visit and Spencer's upset about his parents, the next couple of weeks were reassuringly calm. He seemed to settle with us more and accept how things were, and to embrace the routines we'd put in place. This was key, I felt, to getting him to accept the idea of having boundaries. I even allowed myself to think we were making progress.

John Fulshaw agreed. Spencer was regularly earning all his points now, and when I called John to discuss progress in early October he agreed he could move up to the next level. Spencer was thrilled. This level held the promise of something particularly important: earning points now meant he could buy 'peer time', the opportunity to see friends outside of school.

There was one boy, called Adam, who lived on the street next to ours, with whom Spencer had struck up something of a friendship. He'd obviously not yet been allowed peer time at this point, but had got talking to Adam before the school run every morning, as the local kids tended to congregate outside our house, and I'd recently started allowing him to sit out on the front wall and wait for me. It had been something of a risk after all the nonsense at his own school, but I'd decided to risk it, in order to give him a chance to rebuild trust, and so far it had paid off. He seemed more interested in striking up friendships with the local boys than hotfooting it off down the street.

Because I knew about Adam, I now agreed that for an hour after school every day Spencer could play out not only on our street but also on Adam's, though absolutely nowhere else. I also made clear that time-keeping was key.

'If you're late back,' I explained, still mindful of his history of absconding, 'then there's a very clear consequence in place. The next day you'll lose however many minutes that you were late by, okay?'

Spencer nodded happily, digesting this. Then he frowned. 'But what if I don't realise what the time is, or something?'

I already had this covered. I produced a cheap watch I'd bought for him in town. 'That won't happen,' I told him, 'just as long as you keep this on. It'll also help you with telling the time, won't it?'

'Wow, Casey – thanks!' he said, seeming once again thrilled. 'That's so cool. An' I won't be late, *ever*!'

Spencer, to my delight, was true to his word. Over the next couple of weeks we had a new routine up and running. We'd get back from school around four, and while I made a start on tea he'd go upstairs to change out of his uniform and tidy his bedroom. Having eaten, he'd then be allowed out between five and six, after which he'd come in and get started on his evening routine: pyjamas on, homework, then TV or computer time. And even though I still had my reservations about an eight-year-old being allowed out on the streets unaccompanied – particularly since the nights would soon begin to draw in – it was really encouraging to see things going so well.

However, that wasn't a worry at the weekends. On Saturdays and Sundays the local streets were full of children, and we were able to let Spencer play out earlier in the day. And it continued to go well. I was pleased to see, from the way he chattered on about everyone, that he seemed to make friends quickly and easily. However, the one friendship I was most keen to encourage was a family one; I so wanted him to have a positive relationship with Kieron, who I felt could be such a helpful ally to him. Kieron had been so helpful with previous children we'd fostered, and it still upset me that the incident with Spencer stealing my necklace meant he hadn't bonded with him yet. So one Saturday morning, when I'd planned lunch in town with the kids, I suggested to Spencer that it would be nice if he came with us.

'Oh, but I've planned on playing cops and robbers with my mates today,' he told me.

'That's fine,' I said. 'You can still have your hour playing out. I'd just like you back here by twelve o'clock, that's all, so we can all do something together for a change.'

'Okay,' he said, though not looking entirely convinced that my plan for 'lunch out' would be the highlight of his day. 'I promise. Twelve o'clock,' he agreed, waving the wrist with the watch on. 'So I'd better get going, then, hadn't I?'

Riley had been dropped off by David, and was just coming up the path with the children as Spencer left. 'He's in a rush,' she observed, as he scurried past her to meet the small congregation of kids clustered a few doors down. I explained that I'd asked him to come to town with us, and why.

'I hesitate to tempt fate,' I said as we went into the kitchen for a coffee, 'but I'm really pleased with his progress just lately. It's so good to see him integrating so well with the local kids. It's all happened so much quicker than I'd expected.'

And this *was* unusual. Children in care didn't tend to make friends easily. Even without the psychological problems many of them had, it was difficult, being uprooted from your normal environment, and it took time to build the confidence to make new friends. Riley shook her head, though. 'I'm not surprised at all, Mum. He's hardly like your average eight-year-old, is he? He's so street-wise and worldly, they're all probably in awe of him. And you know how hierarchical children can be – they probably see him as some sort of hero.'

It was a point I hadn't properly considered yet, and in doing so I readily agreed. He probably had all sorts of tales he could brag about, all of which would elevate him in their eyes. Though, where that was concerned, I didn't for a minute imagine what was coming, when there was a sharp rap on the door half an hour later.

It wasn't one rap, either, but a series of bangs. 'Blimey,' I said to Riley, manoeuvring around Levi and Jackson who were playing with some building blocks on the kitchen floor. 'Don't mind my hinges! Who on earth could that be?'

When I opened the door, then, it was something of a shock to see Iris, the elderly lady who lived a few doors down the street, holding her cat, an equally elderly black-and-white tom. The two things didn't stack up – why would she be banging my front door down? – till I saw how red she was in the face. She was clearly furious. And very shaken as well. 'Can I help you, Iris?' I asked her, confused.

In reply, she thrust the cat at me, holding it up at the end of outstretched arms, much to its irritation. It mewed piti-fully. 'What *is* it?' I wanted to know, shocked.

Mike joined me in the hallway, having obviously heard the banging too, even over the din of the sports warm-up programmes that had just started on the TV. Bless him. I knew he'd been hoping for a quiet afternoon.

'It's that boy of yours!' Iris barked, immediately dissolv-ing into tears. 'I caught him red handed, I did. He wants locking up!'

'Spencer?' asked Mike. 'Iris, love, what's he done?'

'Caught him, I did,' she said again. 'Caught him red handed! Swinging Roddy around by his tail, he was. The little … oooh, he's so *cruel*! How could he do a thing like that? He's hurt, you know. Really hurt …' She ground to a halt then, too overcome to continue.

We were both aghast. And appalled. Mike stepped out to scan the street for sight of Spencer, but, perhaps under-standably, he was nowhere to be seen. Indeed, all the kids seemed to have made themselves scarce now. 'I'm so sorry, Iris,' he said. 'This is dreadful, it really is. You're sure it was Spencer?'

'I might be getting on, but I'm not blind, Mr Watson. Oh, it was him all right. I've got his measure, don't you worry. He and that other boy – the one from round the corner. Oh, if I'd caught him … but he saw me coming, and just threw my poor Roddy down … Even laughing, he was. Laughing! He's an evil little brat.'

'I'll go and find him,' Mike started.

'No,' I said. 'Tell you what, I'll go and do that. Why don't you drive Iris round to the emergency vets – see if they can check Roddy over?' I turned to Iris, who was still standing clutching the meowing cat. 'Would that be okay, Iris? Just to be sure he's all right? We'll cover the costs, obviously. Oh, I'm really so, so sorry. This won't be happening again, I promise.'

I felt devastated. Not to mention sick to my stomach. There were all sorts of behaviours that were troubling and distressing, but being wantonly cruel to animals was out there on its own. I recalled what had happened at the farm and felt sicker. As Mike helped Iris and the poor trembling Roddy into the car, I went back inside to fill Riley in properly.

'God!' she said. 'So much for progress then, Mum. And after everything you said to him after that weekend with the Pembertons. Sounds like it's in one ear, and –'

She stopped, stunned into silence. The side door into the kitchen opened, to reveal a grinning Spencer, accompanied by Connor, a boy I recognised from two doors down. 'Oh, hi, Riley,' said Spencer, immediately kneeling down to greet the little ones. 'Hiya, Levi,' he said cheerfully. 'You playing building with your brother?'

I found my voice. 'Spencer, stand up and look at me,' I snapped. He looked shocked and alarmed. In fact, he looked the picture of complete innocence.

'What's up?' he asked.

'I think you know very well, Spencer,' I snapped. 'The lady from down the street has just left here, with Mike. To visit the vets.' I paused a moment, to let this sink in. 'Spencer, she's told us what you did to her cat.'

Now Spencer's expression changed. He looked outraged, and hurt. 'She's blamed *me*?' He glanced at Connor. 'Has she blamed me for what *Adam* did? Has she? I *told* you I'd get the blame!' he protested, looking again at Connor. 'I knew I'd get the blame for it, just cos I was there!'

'Spencer,' I said, cutting through the flow of his indignation. 'She *saw* you. She knows who you are and she saw you. She saw you pick that poor animal up and swing it round by its tail.'

Spencer's eyes filled with tears. 'Connor, tell her!' he shouted. 'Tell her!' he sobbed now. 'Tell her the *truth*!'

I looked at Connor, confused by Spencer's very genuine-seeming anguish. Had Iris got it wrong? 'Well, Connor?' I prompted.

'It wasn't Spence,' he said. 'Honest. It was Adam what done it. We was there, but we didn't do it. We all ran off. It was *Adam*.'

I looked at Riley, whose expression seemed to mirror my own. She shrugged helplessly, as unsure of things as I was.

I turned back to Spencer, whose face was soaked with tears now. 'Spencer,' I said. 'I can't just let this one go. If you're telling me the truth and it *was* Adam who did this, then I'm going to have to go round and see his parents right away. This is serious …'

'So go see them. It *was* him, Casey, honest it was. An' it's about time someone else instead of me got done for everything. He'll prob'ly lie, though. He'll still say it was me.'

'Well, we'll see,' I said. I decided I would go round there right away. So, leaving Riley in charge of Spencer and sending Connor home, I walked round the corner to Adam's house. I needed to get to the bottom of this, however much I cringed at the thought of spelling out what I knew to Adam's poor mum, particularly the implication that it was him who'd been responsible for the despicable deed. It left a bad taste in my mouth.

And as I'd half expected, she'd known nothing and was mortified by the time I'd finished. And when she called Adam into the hallway I caught my breath when I realised how similar, superficially, he looked to Spencer. Same toffee-coloured, curly hair, similar coloured hoodie, same black trackie bottoms … Had Spencer been telling the truth after all? *Was* it a case of mistaken identity? After all, this was a boy I hardly knew.

Adam, as I'd expected, denied everything. In fact, his story was identical to the one I'd already heard. It was just the names of the participants that changed. Yes, he'd been there, he admitted, but it had been Spencer who'd swung the cat round, while he and Connor had stood there and watched him.

I pointed out that Connor had corroborated Spencer's version. 'Course he did,' Adam said, his voice now as indignant as Spencer's had been earlier. 'He's scared of Spencer.' He paused then. 'We *all* are,' he finished.

'And you won't be playing with him any more,' his mother said firmly.

I went home feeling doubly appalled. Appalled to think that Spencer might have done such a dreadful thing, and appalled that, if he *was* lying, he was such a convincing liar. And was he? I couldn't help but suspect so.

Mike called from the vets, shortly after I returned home, to tell me that though Iris's cat was bruised and in shock there was no serious damage that he could see. By now I'd sent Spencer to his room and told him to stay there, and we agreed we'd decide how to play it when Mike got home.

'Please don't say anything to Kieron,' I begged Riley, as I waved her and the kids off to go and meet her brother without me. My own plans for the afternoon were well and truly scuppered, but I didn't want a bad situation made worse than it already was. Kieron was a real animal lover and this incident would horrify him, not to mention also derail my hopes of him warming to Spencer. Happily, Riley understood that, and agreed to keep quiet.

'But don't let this drop, Mum,' she said. 'This kid's clearly got some serious issues going on. You need to get to the bottom of it.'

'I *know*, love,' I said. 'I know.' But *how*, I thought, as I shut the door on my pleasant family afternoon. Now he had a scapegoat to take the rap for him, I felt it highly unlikely Spencer would admit to what he'd done. And if he refused to admit it, then where did I start? How did I find a way to understand the psyche of this troubled child?

And Spencer was, so clearly, profoundly troubled. That was clear. Clear that evening when, his denial meaning nothing had been resolved, we sat down together, as per usual, to do his points.

'Casey,' he asked me, his big brown eyes fixed on mine. 'I can't get grounded for what Adam did, can I? And I've been thinking. You know, about the points for today and that? And I won't lose a load, will I? I mean, I know I'll have to lose *some* – for being there and all. But it won't be *too* many, will it? Because that wouldn't be fair, would it?'

I was speechless. He had clearly gone through all this in his mind, and was now, very coolly, trying to negotiate a deal. I paused, studying the sheet while giving myself time to answer. This child had not only accepted the points system – he positively embraced it. It seemed the accrual of points was his number one concern. But thoughts of the cat? I doubted Roddy had even once crossed his mind. He seemed to be aware of my discomfort as well, leaning across me, as I pondered, to point something out.

'Here,' he said. 'Look. You could take those points off, couldn't you? The ones about behaving sensibly during peer time.'

This was a new category that had been added now that he'd moved to the second level, and, thinking fast, I agreed that those points would indeed have to go. 'But you'll also lose these,' I added, pointing to the ones for respecting adults. 'Because Iris was obviously very distressed about what happened, and though you didn't do it you *were* there. And you didn't try to stop it.'

I watched the smile ebb and then disappear from his face, as it sunk in that he now had insufficient points left to be allowed any peer time the following day.

He said nothing, however. He just drank the remainder of his milk and finished his biscuits in complete silence, and said nothing – not a word to us – as he headed off to bed.

'Not a happy bunny, then?' observed Mike, as we heard his bedroom door closing.

I shook my head. He'd been outmanoeuvred on the points chart and he knew it. Forget the cat, forget remorse, forget his horrible act of cruelty. *He'd* been scuppered, and was very cross. The thought chilled me.

# Chapter 11

Sunday morning saw Spencer once again in a cheerful mood, as if the events of yesterday hadn't even happened. He sat happily down to breakfast, full of chatter about this and that, and tucking into the bacon and eggs I gave him with gusto.

'Hmm,' said Mike, raising a surreptitious eyebrow in my direction. 'You obviously got a good night's sleep, Spencer.'

Spencer nodded. 'I did,' he agreed. 'And now I'm all ready to do whatever you like. I know I'm stopping in today but if you want me to do anything – you know, garden or wash the car or owt – I will do.'

Mike grinned at him. Hard not to – he was such a little charmer. 'Thanks, mate,' he said. 'I'm sure we'll think of something to keep you occupied.'

In the end we spent most of the day baking. It seemed that, like Justin, our first foster child, Spencer was a bit of a dab hand in the kitchen and really enjoyed creating things from scratch. We made a batch of cookies, some butterfly buns and scones and, once they were cooling, even made a casserole together, to have for Sunday dinner, for a change.

There was something about doing things like this together, side by side, which worked its magic on developing a closeness with children, I'd discovered – it seemed to help them open up more than they would if you were talking face to face; something I'd found to be true way back when I'd worked in schools. The horrors of yesterday's cruelty seemed to melt into the distance as Spencer told me a little more about the family he'd come from, how he loved that our house was so warm all the time, compared to his home, which was always so freezing. 'My mum doesn't have the heating on in the daytime,' he told me. 'She says it costs too much, what with seven of us. We always wear a lot of jumpers in the winter.'

He was such a sage little thing in some ways, often sounding older than his years. A real conundrum of a child. But why *was* that?

'Do you help your mum with the cooking, Spencer?' I asked, having shown him how to use the scraper, and watching how deftly he worked his way through all the vegetables.

He shook his head. 'She doesn't do much cooking. Not this kind,' he answered. He stopped then, and finished stripping a carrot of its skin. 'But I'll be able to show her now, won't I? Look, I'm good, me.'

Though I didn't glean much more about what made Spencer tick, it was a good day, a happy day, a day we could build on, and when the kids arrived – Riley and David, Kieron and Lauren – for Sunday dinner, I could see how much it meant to Spencer to have contributed. 'You are *so* clever!' gasped Riley, through a mouthful of casserole. 'Are you renting him out, Mum? I could so do with a chef like Spencer in my house.'

Kieron too seemed warmer towards him, commenting on how tasty his buns were, and I was glad I'd decided not to tell him about the neighbour's cat. However horrible what Spencer had done had been, he was still only eight. Still time for whatever demons caused such dreadful behaviour to be tracked down and pulled out and dealt with. And if there was one thing I was set on, it was doing that.

The next couple of days, too, went remarkably productively. But I wasn't stupid. Spencer was with us for a reason, and a part of me was probably just waiting for that reason to make its presence felt again.

And it did, as expected, the following Wednesday. Not that there was any warning; the day had gone well, Spencer cracking jokes about the shepherd's pie I'd made for dinner, wondering if I'd minced up a bunch of real shepherds and was secretly trying to turn him into a cannibal. And after he'd wolfed it down, I agreed he could have his usual hour of playing out, as he'd earned sufficient points again by now.

'But don't be late, mind,' I warned him as I passed him his watch. 'You don't want to be losing minutes off your tomorrow time, do you?'

Spencer's expression was one of amused resignation. 'I know, Casey,' he said, as if he was 28, rather than eight. 'You tell me every day, and every day I come in on time, don't I?'

'Hey, cheeky face,' I interrupted, 'off you scoot, before I change my mind.'

He grinned impishly as he ran past me to grab his coat.

I smiled to myself as I began clearing the table and preparing a plate of food for Mike, to keep warm in the oven. He'd be home soon, and much preferred that to it being microwaved. That done I made a coffee and grabbed a couple of magazines, keen to catch up with what was happening in the soaps. Ironic, I mused, that since Spencer came I'd fallen behind with most of them. Unlike most of my other kids, he was too young to follow soap operas – no, I thought, he was just like a character from one, instead.

And just as I was thinking it, it seems the fates were keen to prove it, as the silence was broken by a sudden, loud and extremely piercing scream. And not a playful one, either. It was a child's, but it was blood-curdling. I threw down the magazine and rushed to the front door.

My instinct, on opening it, proved to be spot on. Just outside, in full view, and clearly not caring a jot about it, Spencer was beating the living daylights out of a young boy. The child was screaming at him, pleading with him to stop and let him go, but his attempts to crawl away were obviously proving fruitless, Spencer being very much the bigger, stronger one.

And he wasn't letting up. He was kicking and punching the child mercilessly. I flew down the path, horrified, to where they were. 'Spencer,' I yelled, 'what the hell are you doing?' I managed to grab his arm just as he was about to land another vicious punch. 'Spencer! STOP IT! Do you hear me?'

Clearly he didn't. He seemed oblivious. And even as I continued to hold him he continued to kick out. But it was the expression on his face that really chilled me to the bone, it was so strange. His eyes, though on his victim, didn't seem to be 'switched on', somehow, and his mouth was set in a thin rigid line, almost a rictus, which put me in mind again of Justin, who used to have similar sorts of 'turns' when it seemed he'd been consumed by the intensity of his anger.

Thankfully Spencer was a good couple of years younger, so, physically at least, he was no match for me. Though it took almost all my strength, I managed to heave him off the poor lad, who scrambled, terrified, to his feet, and ran away.

I physically carried Spencer back into the house, and, floppy now, he let me. I then deposited him on the sofa in the living room.

Breathless from my exertion I then sat down beside him. 'Right, young man,' I told him. 'You had better start talking. Don't even think of trying the silent treatment with me this time, okay?'

Spencer had now folded his arms across his chest – oozing defiance and defensiveness – and, breathing heavily too, he fixed his eyes on the mirror on the opposite wall. He was flushed and his mouth still had that same linear affect. It was clear he was still struggling to control his anger. Eventually he spoke, the words coming out in staccato bursts. 'He wanted a fight, so I gave him one. I won,' was all he said.

'That's not good enough, Spencer,' I said. 'You were really hurting him. That went way beyond winning. You had completely overpowered him. He was begging you to stop. Who was he, anyway?'

'Aaron,' he said. 'An' I won him fair and square.'

'No, Spencer,' I said. 'There was nothing fair about that fight. Nothing. I won't have it, you hear me? I *saw* what you were doing. That wasn't a fight. That was a beating. And he was *much* smaller than you. I can't believe you're sitting here thinking it was okay to do that. What on earth did he do to deserve treatment like that?'

Now Spencer turned to look at me, visibly calming, if only a little. 'He tried to take Connor and Adam off me,' he told me. 'An' he called me a gay boy!'

Looking at his expression, I could see that this definitely was not the best time to deliver a homily about sticks and stones. 'Well, whatever,' I said. 'You're grounded. And I'd like you to go to your room now. And while you're up there you can use the time to reflect on what you've done. While I speak to Mike. Go on. Go.'

He jumped up, and as he did so I saw his hard expression begin to crumple. 'You're going to send me away now, aren't you? You just want to get rid of me. You do, don't you? Just like my fucking MUM!'

'No, Spencer,' I said firmly, watching his eyes pool with anguished tears. 'Don't be so silly. Of course we don't want to get rid of you. Though you'll be losing more points now, for using bad language, so if you don't want to make things any worse than they are I suggest you do as you're told and get up to that bedroom. And stay there, okay? Now, move it.'

Back in the kitchen I sat down wearily at the table. Was this how he'd always manipulated his parents, perhaps? By doing something wrong and, when they tried to discipline him and teach him the consequences, accuse them of wanting them to be shot of him? If so, then no wonder they were weary and at a loss to know what to do. And where did this anger – this hideously cruel streak – come from? If it was true that the other kids were all behaviourally normal, then why was this kid so challenging to manage? It didn't stack up. Didn't feel logical. And that look on his face had been something to behold. Was it possible he did have some deep-rooted psychological defect, just as his parents had said?

Mike came in moments later, and I told him what had happened and, as ever, he was logic and calm personified – especially in the face of my anxiety about Spencer indeed being born 'not quite right'.

'Love,' he said, 'what's happened isn't evidence of that. Yes, he's a funny lad, and he's clearly got his issues, but he's also a bit of a street kid, it seems to me. I know that sounds ludicrous for an eight-year-old, but it's true. He's clearly been allowed to run wild from an early age, and that's hardened him up, way more so than other children of his age – and this sort of thing is all about territory. Anyway, you don't know the full story, do you? Who knows what this other kid said or did to set him off? There'll be more to it than you think, you wait and see. Boys have scraps. They –'

Mike stopped. The front door had banged. Was still banging – or at least, someone was furiously banging on it. 'Who on earth's doing *that*?' asked Mike incredulously. 'They'll cave the glass in!'

'I'll go,' I said. 'Probably a deputation of kids for him ...'

I left Mike unlacing his boots in the kitchen while I went to tell Spencer's 'friends' that he wouldn't be coming out again today. Or tomorrow, or the day after ...

But it wasn't a gang of children. It was one woman. One very angry woman in her twenties, who looked as if she was ready to kill.

'Would you like me to kick *your* fucking head in?' she raged at me, stabbing her finger threateningly close to my face. 'You keep that fucking animal away from my son,' she screamed at me, 'or believe me, I will come back and I'll fucking kill you!'

Mike, obviously hearing her, was by my side in seconds. 'Do you mind!' he snapped. 'My wife has done absolutely nothing wrong. So I'd be grateful if you could speak to her a bit more civilly. Now, do you want to come inside and discuss this calmly? I'm assuming your Aaron's mum?' He paused. 'Though it's up to you, obviously ...'

The woman's expression showed no sign of softening. She was just much, much too angry and a part of me wondered if I wouldn't be the same in such circumstances with my own kids.

'Yes, I'm fucking Aaron's mum and no I don't want to fucking come in! You –' she stabbed the finger again, this time at Mike. 'You want to control your kid a bit better, you hear me? And, while I'm at it, you'll also be getting a bill for my son's glasses.'

'Glasses?' Mike asked.

'Yes, glasses!' the woman snapped. 'The glasses your son decided to smash before he beat my son up!'

Our expressions were obviously clear to her. 'Oh, didn't tell you that bit, did he? Oh, yes, lovely kid, he is. Took them off him and jumped up and down on them. Even told him he was "fucking blind now!" You're lucky I'm not going to the cops with this, trust me. I still might. You're going to pay for those glasses, you hear me?'

I stood, dazed and appalled, as Mike tried to calm the woman down. I listened as he explained that Spencer was in care, that he was a troubled child and that we were his temporary foster carers, that we were doing our best and that this definitely wouldn't be happening again. And that, of *course*, we would pay for new glasses.

He might as well have been talking to her in Serbo-Croat.

'Great,' she said. 'Fucking great! So we all just have to put up with that, do we? Fucking council. Sending kids like that to live with decent people. We should be *told* people like you live on our streets.'

Mike did a brilliant job in keeping his cool. He just continued to apologise to the woman, until, eventually, she huffed off down the path. But I was really upset. Really properly upset. To think people would see us not as doing our best, but as nuisance neighbours. Pariahs. That really hurt me. Little did I know that, when it came to falling out with all the neighbours, in taking on Spencer we'd hardly scratched the surface.

# Chapter 12

Because of the severity of Spencer's actions, we did ground him, and this time there would be no discussions about his points chart – we decided to keep him in for a whole week.

Not that he put up any sort of argument. When we told him he didn't try to negotiate his way out of it, or lessen the 'sentence', just accepted it meekly and apologetically. He also tried hard to be extra well behaved. He spent the next few days coming in from school and playing quietly with jigsaws and board games with me, and by the time the weekend came around he'd still not so much as even asked when he might next be allowed to play out.

Spencer also seemed keen to show us how much it mattered that he get back into our good books again. On the following Saturday he positively threw himself into the task of helping Mike clear out the shed. It was a horrible job, and one that turned up, like a bad penny, every autumn. Year in year out, it was always the same. We'd spend most of the year filling it with the usual family detritus: broken bikes, broken lawn mowers, broken toys and appliances, plus all the boxes that had contained their replacements. Mike would then insist, every year, that we clear it all out, in order that we could start refilling it after Christmas with the next round of discarded stuff that was too big for the bins and which had been edged out of commission by Santa Claus.

Spencer took to this job with real gusto. I didn't know quite how he felt about the impending festivities, much less how he felt about where he might be, but he threw himself into it, declaring himself not at all afraid of spiders, and despite all that had happened recently my heart went out to him.

But he really stunned us by his announcement a couple of evenings later. Perhaps – just perhaps – we were turning a corner after all.

'Casey, Mike,' he said, as the three of us sat down to eat our tea, 'can I talk to you both for a minute?'

'Oh-oh, that sounds serious,' joked Mike, putting down his cutlery. 'Come on, then. What have we done wrong?'

Spencer giggled and gave Mike a playful punch on the arm. 'It's not that,' he said. 'It's that I've been thinking. You know, about what a proper pain in the butt I've been lately, and everything.'

Mike looked at him, wide-eyed. '*You*, Spence? Surely not.'

'Oh, Mi-ike!' Spencer moaned. 'Casey, *tell* him.'

'Shh, Mike,' I said. 'Let poor Spencer speak.'

Mike apologised. 'Go on, then, lad,' he said.

'Well, like I was saying,' Spencer went on, 'I've been a right pain, haven't I? So I've decided that instead of going to bed at seven, like I'm supposed to, I'm going to go at six. You know, so's you can have a bit more time together. A bit more peace.'

'Oh, Spencer,' I said, touched, even though a teeny cynical bit of me was waiting for the deal-making 'and if' that must surely follow it. 'That's really very thoughtful of you, but six o'clock is way too early for you to be going to bed. There's no need, honest. And besides, we like having time with you. We wouldn't do this job if we didn't, would we?'

His tone was firm, however, when he answered. 'I've made up my mind,' he said. 'I'm off to bed at six, starting from tonight. I won't go to sleep or anything. I'll just read or something, till I'm tired. You *deserve* it.'

His expression was so sweet and sincere that even though the cynical part was still nudging me for attention I didn't have the heart to turn down his offer. Who cared that it might be to butter us up for some as yet undisclosed reason? If it turned out that it was because he wanted to wheedle an extra half hour's peer time once he was allowed to go out and play again, then was that such a bad thing anyway? Better to learn give and take – better to learn that doing nice things for people usually made them think well of you – than to rail against boundaries and think you could do just as you liked. No, this was fine. 'Well, thank you for thinking about us,' I said. 'That's very thoughtful, Spencer.'

Even so, for the next couple of nights I would sneak up and listen outside his bedroom door, wondering exactly what he might be up to. I didn't imagine he'd go back to gouging holes in his bedroom walls, but, well, given the circumstances, I just couldn't help but feel suspicious.

But after four days in which nothing untoward seemed to be happening – no suspicious noises, no hint of mischief – Mike told me to calm down and just accept it for what it was: Spencer's way of showing us he was trying to be good for us. And, as I'd said, even if he did have ulterior motives, better this than thieving or getting angry, or running away. Bless him, I decided. This *was* progress.

But on the fifth night the true extent of our naivety was about to hit us squarely in the face.

I'd just sat down to watch *EastEnders* when the doorbell rang. I'd been looking forward to it, too, having not caught up with it for so long. At first I thought it might be Kieron, who'd mentioned something about coming around to use our printer during the week. But then I decided it couldn't be. Kieron was too routine-obsessed for that. He'd have called and texted first to make sure not only that we were home, but also that there was definitely ink and paper.

'Watch carefully, and tell me anything I miss,' I ordered Mike, as I got up from the sofa and went out into the hall. Once there, I then unlocked and opened the door. And then froze. I couldn't quite take in the reality of what I was seeing, which was an angry-looking man I didn't recognise holding by the scruff of his scrawny eight-year-old neck an equally angry-looking Spencer.

It took me several seconds to even *think* about speaking. This just couldn't *be*. He'd gone to bed. The doors were locked. How could he be standing on my front doorstep? Wriggling on my front doorstep, in fact.

'What?' I finally managed. 'I don't understand ... what's going on?'

The man was quick to supply me with an answer. 'I've just caught this little *prat* in my *bedroom* is what's going on,' he said. 'Going through my stuff. Almost got away with it, too, didn't you?' He glared down at Spencer. 'Except he didn't count on my wife being in the en suite at the time, did you?' Now he also gave Spencer a little shake.

As had happened only so very recently, Mike had heard the man's raised voice, and, once again, had come to join me at the door. He looked as stupefied as I had, his gaze darting from the man to me to Spencer.

'He's been in their bedroom,' was all I could manage to say.

'Thieving!' the man added, for good measure.

'You!' barked Mike. 'Inside with Casey. Right away.'

His tone was obviously sufficiently strong that the man released Spencer, presumably satisfied Mike would give him the sort of hiding he deemed appropriate. Spencer shot in and I hurried with him back into the living room. I shut the door on the two men, who were having a heated exchange now, and also the TV and my quiet half hour in Albert Square.

Once again, a cynical part of me couldn't help but observe that in Spencer we had a ready-made plot line. But the enormity of what he'd done meant my wry humour was quickly gone. I put my hands on my hips and reconfigured my face into an angry frown. Neither was difficult. I was absolutely furious.

'Spill,' I commanded. 'No lies. No excuses. No justifications. You've been caught, so there's nothing you can say that will get you out of this. The *whole* truth. I need to know *everything*.'

He'd barely opened his mouth when Mike came back in and joined us. 'And it had better be the truth, mind,' he told him. 'Better match up *exactly* to what I've just been told or you'll find yourself grounded till you're 16. I mean it!'

And, outmanoeuvred, Spencer did tell us everything. Pretty much every night, since the first night of his six o'clock, self-imposed, terribly thoughtful curfew, Spencer had been climbing out of his skylight, crawling across our roof, shimmying down a drainpipe onto the roof of the (now beautifully tidy) shed, and from there scampering across a fence into the next street. There he'd been meeting up with a seven-year-old boy – another one he'd recently befriended.

They too had a shed, and, with another bout of gymnastics, he'd then been climbing into the boy's bedroom. From here he had been on a number of sorties, wandering around much of the upstairs, snooping for things he might pinch.

Tonight, however, he had finally been scuppered. He'd gone into the boy's parents' room and, seeing a pair of discarded jeans on the floor, had set about checking all the pockets in the hopes of finding money. At this point the boy's mother had emerged from the en suite and had caught him both red faced and red handed.

Bizarrely, the first thought that crossed my mind as Spencer admitted this was that I hoped she had her modesty covered.

'I can barely believe what you've just told us,' I spluttered. And I couldn't. I was simply lost for words. Quite apart from the danger of playing *Mission Impossible* on the neighbourhood roofs and fences, how on earth had Spencer managed to persuade the boy in the next street to let him do that? Not climbing into his bedroom – to an impressionable seven-year-old, I could see it might all seem rather exciting – but to give him carte blanche to simply saunter round his house? It beggared belief. But then, did it? Where Spencer was concerned, I was rapidly re-writing the credibility handbook. His latest escapade sounded so cartoonish it was almost funny. Except it wasn't. It wasn't funny at all. He could have been seriously injured, or even killed!

'You silly, *silly* boy!' I berated him now. 'Do you not realise how dangerous what you've been doing was? You were risking your life. What were you *thinking*?' My voice had gone up a couple of octaves as the full implication began to hit me. I was also very angry. Where did I start with this child?

'What do you care?' Spencer answered, in a much calmer voice than I'd managed. 'Anyway, I'm like a spy, like that man on *Mission Impossible*. I can run just as well on rooftops as most people can on the ground.'

That he'd mentioned the same movie I'd thought of hit home for me. He really did seem to think that. He was deadly serious. He meant it.

'Spencer, that's a really silly, childish thing to say. You know full well that what you see in the movies is all made-up stuff. You know better than that!' I snapped.

I brought myself up short then. Did he? Did he really? And why wouldn't he say childish things? He *was* a child. He seemed so streetwise, so sassy and so big for his age that I kept forgetting that this was a little boy of *eight*.

Mike could obviously see we'd get nowhere. Not tonight, anyway. 'Go back to bed, Spencer,' he said wearily. 'Just go back to bed, and *stay there*. We'll deal with all this in the morning. And that window, as well … Go on. Hop it!'

Mike's voice seemed to jerk Spencer's brain to a new place. Head now lowered submissively, he crossed the room, then stopped and turned in the doorway, looking once again like the troubled, vulnerable little boy he really was.

'Mike, d'you swear on me mother's life that you won't send me away again?'

Mike sighed heavily. 'It's a bit late to be worrying about that, isn't it, lad? But no, Spencer. That's not the plan. Never was. Now get to bed.'

Spencer nodded and disappeared off up the stairs.

'God,' I said, once he'd gone, 'what on earth are we going to *do* with this child?'

'Call John, I think, love. Get some advice from him in the morning. The guy from *Mission Impossible*?' He shook his head. 'What next?'

I smiled, but the reality of Spencer's flights of fancy was very serious. 'I'm hoping he'll agree we can just ground him until further notice.'

Mike shook his head. 'Yes, and I'll pop down to the DIY store and see if I can knock up a cell, shall I? Can't see how else we're going to keep him indoors, can you? Come on. Must be nearly time for *Police, Camera, Action!* Perhaps we can pick up a few tips …'

Happily, John agreed that the best thing would be for us to keep Spencer under house arrest (not his words, but definitely how it was beginning to feel) until he could come up for a proper progress meeting the following Friday. 'And let's see how the next contact visit goes, as well, shall we?' he added. 'Which I was going to call you about anyway. Will next Saturday work for you two?'

I checked the calendar on the kitchen wall as I spoke to him. 'Yes, that's fine,' I said, pencilling it in. 'Well, at least I *hope* it will be …'

'I'm sure some lessons have been learned there,' John chuckled.

'Honestly,' I said. 'You are *such* an optimist, John.'

'Only thing to be in my line of work,' he countered. 'Speaking of which, there's one other thing on my "things to nag Casey about" list.'

'Oh-oh. I'm not liking the sound of that.'

'But I'm going to nag you about it even so. The next agency social. Couple of days away. You'll have already had the flyer. Look, I know I bang on about them endlessly, but it's not just to drag up the numbers. I think it would be really useful for you and Mike to attend.'

'Still not liking the sound of that, John …'

'I know it's not your sort of thing,' he said. 'Honestly, but can't you give it a try? Honestly, I think you'd enjoy it. Much more than you think you will. Almost all of the other specialist carers are going to be there, and, well, you know … a problem shared is a problem halved and all that. It would be good for you to chat with others in your shoes.'

John was spot on. It wasn't my sort of thing. Well, not up to now, at any rate. I knew I was probably being silly, but since I'd started fostering I'd always felt a little bit intimidated by the other carers I'd encountered. They all seemed to be so, well, posh, I suppose. Where my own roots were unashamedly working class, they had tended to come from professional backgrounds like teaching, psychology and positions in the police force, because those were the places where most of the recruitment was done. It wasn't so much that I felt judged by them, just that I wasn't one of them. I was also – still am – quite a private person, really, and had never, truth be known, felt the need. But I took the point. When you worked at such a challenging job, pooling experiences and advice made good sense. 'I know,' I said guiltily. 'I did get the invite and everything. It's just that we've been so busy lately and …'

'Casey, so's everyone else. *Please* come. Give it whirl. I know you'll enjoy it.'

So that was me told. And he was right. We really *should* make the effort. Even if only to confirm that it wasn't our sort of thing. And as soon as we arrived – at the agency's function suite, which was the venue – I immediately felt exactly as I'd expected I probably would: anxious, intimidated and overdressed. It hadn't been flagged up as anything particularly grand, but conscious that I wanted to make a good impression I'd made Mike, who'd taken a half day's leave from work, wear a suit – despite his protests – and had dressed myself in a fitted black dress and *faux*-fur coat. Mike's face fell even further than mine, if that were possible, as we scanned the room to see a sea of jeans and jumpers. 'Great,' Mike hissed. 'Now I look like a right berk.'

'Well, how was *I* to know?' I hissed back, as we plastered smiles on our faces and prepared to make our entrance.

'Just don't attempt to do your posh voice,' he retorted, through gritted teeth.

I don't know if he could see our discomfort at 40 paces, but John suddenly appeared, as if from nowhere.

'Oh, look at you,' he said. 'Very nice.' Which I knew would make Mike squirm. But I for one was pleased to see him. I felt much less exposed with him by my side. 'Come on,' he said, 'let's mingle. Oh. You'll remember Annie, of course, won't you?' He pointed. 'See, she's just over there. We've got a couple of our mainstream carers here today, as well, and I'm pretty sure you'll recognise a few of them.'

He bustled us around then, introducing us to various people, and it became obvious that these socials were generally well attended. Pretty much everyone seemed to know everyone else. Except us. John was right. I should really make the effort to come more. Yes, it was tiring doing an endless round of smiling and small talk, but it was silly to miss a chance to catch up with fellow carers, and with my nest at home – bar the children we fostered, of course – empty, it was sensible to expand our social network.

And we really couldn't have been made more welcome. It was a good half hour before we had a chance to sit down with coffees. And Annie, spotting us again, immediately came and joined us.

'How are things going with the delightful Spencer,' she asked us, sitting down.

'Oh, much as you'd expect, I imagine,' I told her, remembering her warning to us on that first day.

She smiled ruefully. 'I wanted to warn you,' she said. 'Though I obviously didn't want to ladle it on too thick.'

I thought back. What part of 'he's like no child I've ever met before' was ladling it on thinly? But no matter. She'd probably forgotten her exact words in any case.

'Judging from the fun and games we've had with him, you must have had a pretty tough time,' Mike suggested.

'You're not kidding,' she said. 'And I did hold back, if I'm honest, because it was so important someone take him. The alternative would have been a children's home, and none of us ever want that, do we?'

We both shook our heads. Last chance saloon, that was our house.

'But sometimes you have to be clear-headed about these kids, don't you? For your own protection. Did John tell you about the knife incident?' she then said, bringing my musings to a halt.

'What knife incident?' asked Mike.

'Ah, apparently not, then.'

'But what happened?' I asked, revisiting uncomfortable memories with Justin, who, in the early weeks of living with us, had threatened me with one.

'Took one of my kitchen knives and went on a rampage, the little sod.'

'You mean he *attacked* you?' I said, shocked. I simply couldn't see Spencer doing that. But then, there'd been lots of things that hadn't seemed likely when we'd first met him. 'Surely we should have known about something like that?' I said.

But she shook her head. 'No, no, not me, thank goodness. Sorry, I should have phrased that a bit less alarmingly, shouldn't I? No, just the house and garden. But that was bad enough. Slashed my furniture, beheaded half the flowers in my flowerbeds. Bored, that was all. He was bored and cross because he couldn't play out. Just lost it completely. In the end I just had to leave him out there. Leave him to it. Leave him to decimate whatever he could decimate, until he'd worn himself out and had enough. But it was the last straw. He was really far too much for a lone carer. Well, *this* lone carer, at any rate.' She smiled thinly. She did look exhausted. 'Though I'm sure you two are able to manage him a lot better. You know, man in the house, and all that.'

'We should have been *told*,' I said to Mike, as Annie went off to speak to another carer.

'Well, there's John,' he said, pointing. He was standing a few feet away. 'Let's ask him why we weren't, since we're here.'

'It wasn't *that* bad,' John told us, once we'd flagged him down and asked him. 'To be honest, it was only a tiny nick in her sofa. She does tend to over-dramatise,' he added, lowering his voice a bit. 'Honestly, it was really no big deal, just a bit of a childish tantrum. I didn't even know about it till a couple of weeks after he left her. I think she just wanted to claim for a new sofa, to be honest. Not that she isn't *entirely* justified in doing so, of course.'

And it wasn't just Annie's revelations that made it seem worthwhile to have gone to the social. The rest of the morning, too, proved to be fruitful. We had a guest speaker come to talk to us about fostering children on the autistic spectrum, which was particularly interesting for us, as parents of a child who had Asperger's. I liked to keep up to date on new research and was always ravenous for new information about the condition; there'd been such a profound lack of that when Kieron had been growing up. It would also prove useful, I knew, if, as specialist carers, we were asked to care for children with such complex needs. And with more and more kids diagnosed, and getting support now, that was obviously a possibility. Kids on the autism spectrum threw up challenges for the most committed of parents, so when they were born into families that were chaotic and already struggling they often bore the brunt of the dysfunction. Listening to the speaker, it occurred to me that I'd really relish that kind of challenge, as I realised I wasn't the poor relation to all these professionals, and neither was Mike. We'd actually developed a really useful set of fostering skills between us, which we could put to good use if we were called upon.

Right now, however, a child with complex needs was already in residence, and I felt a little spark of defensiveness about the way Annie had described him. A sure sign an emotional bond was forming in me. Whatever the challenges *he* threw up over the coming weeks, our little Tom Cruise/Houdini hybrid could count on us.

We picked Spencer up from school on the way home from the social and decided, as a treat, to take him to McDonald's for tea. It would both save me cooking and give us another chance, in neutral surroundings, to talk to him a little more about his behaviour. I explained that John would be coming to visit and would probably like a chat with him, and that he'd be round on Friday evening, after school.

Spencer looked shocked.

'But how come? I'm going to see Mum and Dad this weekend, aren't I?'

'Yes, you are, love,' I said. 'But that's not till Saturday.'

He looked upset now. 'But I thought I was going for the whole weekend.'

I had no idea where he'd got this from. Wishful thinking, no doubt. And selective memory, too, after what had happened last time. 'No, darling,' I said, glancing at Mike. 'It's a day visit. Remember how we said that if the day visits went well we could then talk about going for a sleepover?' I looked carefully at Spencer, and could almost see him analysing my words.

'No,' he said, firmly, 'I *don't* remember that. I went to all that trouble last time to stay out of their way, an' now you're saying it was all for nowt?'

Now he sounded like he was about to cry.

This brought me up short. What on earth was he on about? 'What do you mean, love, you went to all what trouble?' Again, I was confused by the way his mind worked. 'You mean when you ran away?'

Spencer looked at me and Mike with an expression that seemed to say there was no point in him even trying to explain. He stood up then, his chin wobbling, and, having glanced around to check where it was, pushed his tray away and started towards the toilets. I was about to speak, but Mike placed a hand over mine and I realised Spencer's silence was because he was wrestling with his emotions. He would hate to cry in public, I knew.

'What d'you think he means?' I asked Mike, once he'd gone. 'About staying out of their way?'

'What he says, I suppose,' he said, shaking his head. 'There's clearly more to all this, isn't there?'

I nodded. 'There's definitely something he's not telling us ... and, oh God,' I said, suddenly panicked. 'There isn't a back door to this place that he could slip out of, is there? Be just great if he –'

But my panic was mercifully short-lived. Spencer re-emerged at that moment, looking a little more composed.

'Spencer, what do you mean, love?' I persisted gently, once he'd sat down again. 'Are you saying you *didn't* run away last time you went home? What?'

He stared down at the remains of his tea for a moment. 'I swear, Casey,' he said, finally. 'If they don't want me back this time, I'm gonna kill me mum – I am! She *swore* to me that this was only gonna be for a bit. Till things settled down. She just better want me back this time. I mean it.'

With that he stood up again, turned from the table, and this time headed straight for the restaurant's front door. Mike followed, while I quickly cleared up and returned the tray. There'd been no doubt and no discussion when this little boy had come to us. No indication that anything wasn't as it seemed. It had been taken as a given. Spencer, by his own admission, had put *himself* into care. It had been entirely at his instigation. Yes, the parents had agreed to it; said they realised it was for the best. But because of what *he'd* done. Or was it?

I felt a familiar sniff of intrigue, alongside one of growing anger. Could it be true? Had this whole sorry business been put in motion by Spencer's mother? Had she actually encouraged her own child to put himself into care? Made some sort of deal with him about it?

I pulled the door open and followed them both out into the car park. I needed to find myself some answers.

# Chapter 13

The rest of the week passed without any major blow-ups or incidents, and I resisted the urge to quiz Spencer further about the things he'd let slip in McDonald's. I had a hunch, and Mike agreed, that to push it would be counter-productive. There was clearly more going on than social services knew, but the answer was not to interrogate Spencer, but to be receptive to what might come out after his next visit, which was going to be happening in a couple of days anyway.

Spencer himself definitely seemed much more subdued than normal, either because he was anxious about John visiting, or about seeing his parents – perhaps both. And I was grateful, as awful as it sounded to admit it, as it meant he seemed to prefer to stay in after school, rather than endlessly trying to interrogate *me* about why he couldn't play out with his friends.

On the Friday, knowing John would be arriving as soon as we were back, I took some snacks to school when I drove to pick up Spencer. 'Here you go, love,' I told him as he climbed into the back seat and passed him the plastic box. 'There's some sandwiches and fruit in there for you. You know by now just how long meetings can drag on for, and I thought you might be too hungry to wait for a cooked tea.'

He tucked in immediately – he'd never lacked appetite – but I could still sense his instant anxiety. 'It's not going to be proper long, is it? Proper long meetings make me proper, proper tired.'

I smiled. He was sounding like a little old man. 'I shouldn't think so, love,' I told him. 'Not "proper" long. I think John just wants to talk to you about how we can all help you when you start to get angry thoughts about things. You know – to give you suggestions to use, so that you can think before you act and make good choices.'

He frowned. 'You mean tell me how to stop being bad?'

'Kind of, I suppose, but you know, Spencer, it's not really *you* that's bad. Inside I know that there's a really lovely little boy. It's just that it's hard for us to see him sometimes, isn't it? Because the things you sometimes choose to do make you *look* bad. But it's the behaviours that are bad, Spencer, not you.'

He chewed thoughtfully for a few minutes before he replied. He was such a thinker. Always seemed to consider everything said to him. Something that, one day, would stand him in good stead – if he was given the chance to shine, at any rate. 'Right,' he said eventually. 'So will John tell my mum and dad that it's okay that I do bad stuff, cos it's not really my fault – it's just because I have behaviours?'

'That's not *quite* how it works, love,' I said gently, but still firmly. Knowing Spencer as I did now, I wasn't sure if he was trying to turn this to his advantage, or that he genuinely didn't understand what I meant. 'What we all want to do – what we all *need* to do – is to help stop you from acting out these behaviours. Stop the running away. Stop the taking things. Stop the hurting people. We want you to start making better choices about what you do. That way it will be you – not any of us, *you* – who decides what kind of boy Spencer really is and wants to be. Do you understand that?'

He thought again. 'I think so.' Then he sighed. 'But can we have the Chipmunks now, please? I've got a headache.'

I smiled. So that was me told.

As I'd expected, when we pulled into the drive John was already parked up and sitting in his car, waiting for us. He followed us into the house, trying to engage Spencer in a chat about how his day at the agency had gone. Spencer, I could see, was fast running out of interest, and I realised he was also hopping from foot to foot. But it wasn't until John paused for breath between anecdotes that Spencer interrupted him, grinning shyly. 'Sorry, John,' he said politely, 'I'd like to stay and hear more about your lost diary, honest, but I'm busting for a wee. I gotta go.'

With that he shot inside and bolted straight up the stairs, leaving John in the hall, staring after him, bemused.

'Come on,' I said. 'Let me get the kettle on, while he gets changed out of his uniform.'

John followed me into the kitchen. 'Quite the little charmer, isn't he?'

'He's in one of his good moods,' I told him. 'So you're lucky. And I was thinking. It's probably best if I don't join you. He always seems better one on one – I think you're likely to get more out of him. Plus I think he'll take things more seriously if it feels a bit "official", so I thought you could take him into the living room to chat while I get on with making Mike's tea.'

John agreed, but when Spencer came down, in his favourite rugby shirt and a pair of joggers, he looked surprised and a little panicky that I wasn't to be included. I ruffled his hair and reassured him. 'No need for me, today,' I told him. 'Go on – you'll be fine.'

He didn't look convinced, and John's carefully crafted 'stern' face clearly worried him. But that was good, I thought. He needed to be more fearful of authority. Of the consequences of actions. It wasn't rocket science.

Having settled them in the living room, I returned to the kitchen to prepare tea. I'd decided upon tacos and salad – a new family favourite that had been visited on us, as ever, by Kieron, for whom it was the 'for the moment' food of choice. Kieron went through phases with foods, always had. When he found something he liked, he would want to eat it daily, and this would go on until he – not to mention the rest of us – grew sick of it. As a mother, when he was young, this had been something of a challenge, but these days it was more of an inspiration to be more adventurous, because Kieron wouldn't rest until every member of the family had tried whatever his latest obsession was.

With no idea how long John would be chatting to Spencer, I prepped everything but resisted the urge to start cooking. Mike would be home soon but they might be in there for an hour. As it was, though, only 20 minutes passed before I heard the door open, disgorging only John.

'All's well,' he said, in response to my enquiring expression. 'I just wanted to check something with you. I've agreed he can start going out to play again next week – provided you're happy that he has sufficient points, obviously – but I wondered if you'd agree to him having half an hour today, while we have a chat. A gesture of trust, I thought.'

'Of course,' I said. 'Now?'

John nodded. 'Spencer!' At which he was out like a shot, almost knocking me over in a clumsy and unexpected hug. 'Aw, thanks, Casey. I promise I'll be good and come back an' that. Just half an hour, okay? Don't you worry!'

'He seems really determined to try and be good,' John said, once I'd poured us both another coffee and we'd sat down at the dining table. 'He's agreed to seeing a support worker once a week, which is great. Penny Creswell – have you come across her?' I shook my head. 'She's great. Background in psychology and lots of experience working with kids with anger management problems, so I think it'll be a good match.'

'That's good news,' I agreed. 'What else did you cover?'

'Oh, probably pretty much the same sort of thing as you. Just tried to get across how he's got to rein in. How easy it would be to get a name with the police, and how damaging that could be for his future. Plus the dangers he faces by running off on his own all the time, on which point I think I hammered my point home pretty well. It's funny, though

– I had to keep reminding myself he's only eight. Sometimes it felt like I was talking to a young teenager.'

*No shit, Sherlock!* I thought, but obviously didn't say. 'Tell me about it,' I responded instead. 'But what about tomorrow? His home visit. Did you cover that at all? We spoke about it earlier in the week and he seemed genuinely convinced he was going for a sleepover.'

'I know,' John replied. 'And we discussed all that at length. I think I've managed to impress upon him how that's only going to happen if he can prove to us he can be grown up and responsible – no runners – before we can even *go* there.'

'There's something else,' I said. 'Something that's been playing on my mind. When I told him it wasn't going to be sleepovers for a while yet, he was really upset – upset that he'd been good and got out from under his mum's feet. Not run off at all – just "got out from under her feet". He also intimated that coming into care was something he'd agreed to, not instigated. I feel sure there's something going on with that family that we don't know. That there's more than this "out of control kid" thing going on. I don't want to start interrogating him, but I'm sure there's something major going on with his mother that he's not telling us. What d'you think?'

John spread his palms. 'I probably know less about them than you do, to be honest. They've never been known to social services, so there's nothing on file. Shall I have a word with Glenn?'

'I'd be grateful,' I said. 'I'm just worried his mum is manipulating him in some way. And if she does have a drink problem, then …'

'A drink problem? Is that on record? I wasn't aware …'

'No, no. Well, not as far as I know. Sorry, John. I hadn't mentioned that to you, had I? And I'm not even sure it should *be* on record. I don't want to throw accusations around without facts. It's just that, between you and me, when we dropped Spencer off there the last time, well, Kerry just appeared to be a bit out of sorts, and well, we could smell the alcohol on her at the door. It might have been a one-off, of course, but it's just something that Mike and I discussed as a possibility. I'm not sure –'

The side door slammed then, so I shut up, and John drained his coffee. 'Leave it with me,' he said as Spencer bounced in, grinning and red faced.

'See. I told you!' he beamed, obviously proud of himself. He lifted the wrist with his watch on. 'Connor begged me to stay out a bit longer, but I said no. I told him, "Connor, I have to go in now. You'll just have to play with someone else till the next time." He didn't like it –' Spencer now spread his own palms, theatrically, as he glanced at us in turn. 'But what can you do?'

John laughed out loud as he stood up to put on his coat. 'Such a caring soul, you are, Spence. And a human dynamo to boot! Wish I had your energy on a Friday afternoon. Next time I'm up, perhaps we can have a kick-about together, eh? I'd like a dose of whatever it is you're running on! Something I could bottle, to see me through the week.'

Spencer beamed at this, and I felt a real surge of positivity. Which could have done with bottling as well, as it turned out, and then laid down, like a fine wine, to keep in reserve for later. I should have realised it wasn't going to last.

Saturday morning, however, saw us still full of hope, as we arrived at Spencer's parents' house bright and early. Not that it was bright. It was actually a pretty damp late October morning, the sort of day that seems to presage the gloom of the coming winter, but is still too far away from Christmas to feel even vaguely festive. Just grey and grim and cheerless, the trees devoid of colour, their leaves a soggy brown carpet on the ground.

Spencer, however, was in high spirits – had been since the previous evening – and ran eagerly up the path to where his dad waited at the door. 'Hi, Dad,' he said brightly, pushing past him. 'Where's Mum?'

His dad laughed and shook his head. 'Now there's one eager beaver!' he said cheerfully. 'He seems in a good mood,' he observed as Spencer disappeared down the hall.

'It's been a good week,' I confirmed. 'It really does feel as if we're making progress. He's –'

'And long may it continue,' Spencer's dad answered, interrupting me. 'Right, four o'clock again, is it?'

Mike had barely inclined his head in a confirming nod before Spencer's father had stepped back inside, almost shutting the door in our faces.

'That's one strange family,' Mike whispered as we went back down the path, both a bit shocked at the abruptness of our parting. 'He's all so jolly, and then, whump, we've been dismissed. But come on, let's make the most of our time off

145

today, shall we?' He rubbed his hands together. 'B&Q, here we come …'

I pulled a face at this. DIY stores weren't much of a highlight in my life. I suppose we were a pretty traditional couple. Mike loved looking at drills and other stupid things like that, whereas I loved nothing better than to shop for clothes and handbags. But I had to let him have his turn occasionally, I conceded. In fact I'd agreed much less reluctantly than I might have, based on a thought that had occurred to me. At this time of year all the big DIY superstores gave over loads of floor space to Christmas decorations, and if there was one thing I loved as much as shopping for food and handbags, it was Christmas and all that went with it. So I was happier than I might have been. Quite jaunty, in fact. I could immerse myself in fairy lights while he pored over power tools. Every cloud, and all that, I thought, as I climbed into the car.

I was also confident that John's feelings about Spencer were right, that he understood now how important this visit was going to be. So it was in a completely chilled mood, after a lovely, relaxing lunch, that I climbed out of the car again, on our return, on the dot of four.

It was a mood that would be shattered in an instant.

Danny Herrington was already standing on the doorstep, and in stark contrast to his sunny disposition when we'd dropped Spencer that morning he now stood there grim faced, arms folded, with the door shut behind him. What was it about this man and his reluctance to open his front door? What was his house – Fort bloody Knox? Which thought put another thought – a bad one – in my head. We hurried up the path to see him clutching a piece of paper, which, as we approached him, he thrust out towards us.

'What's wrong?' asked Mike, striding up to him. 'Where's Spencer?'

'You've to ring that number,' he said. 'It's the police. They're expecting to hear from you. Spencer ran off half an hour back.'

His expression was stony. Clearly something bad had happened.

'What?' I said. 'I don't believe this. He was so happy to be coming home today. What on earth happened to make him run off again?'

Once again I was conscious of the lack of Spencer's mother. Where was she right now, come to that? And what was her part in all this?

'I'm sorry, Mrs Watson,' Spencer's father said, frowning. 'It was quite serious, I'm afraid. I had to call the police myself.'

'*Call* the police? What, because of something he'd done? Why on earth –' Mike began, as stunned as I was.

'I'm afraid he attacked his mother. Quite violently. I can't be having that. Not in front of the other kids, can I? Hit on the head. With a brick …'

I realised suddenly that he seemed to be trying not to cry, that the stony expression was just a product of him trying to hold himself together. Oh God, I thought, suddenly feeling so sorry for the man. The whole family. The other kids … I simply couldn't understand it.

'What happened?' I asked again, this time more gently. 'Mike, love, why don't you get on and give the police our number?'

'It all happened so fast,' Spencer's dad said. 'He was out in the garden playing with Coral and Harvey – they're our youngest – and he must have picked the stone up and –'

'Stone?' I said, feeling more hopeful. 'Not a brick?'

'Well, half a brick,' he said. 'I've been doing some work in the garden. And, well, I don't know what caused it, but next thing I knew, all hell had broken loose in the kitchen – Kerry had called them all in for squash and biscuits. And he was having a right go at his mother – goodness knows why. So I stepped in to try and calm him down, and next thing I know he's pulled this brick out and smashed her over the head with it. He was off then, of course.' Danny Herrington sighed deeply. 'Down the garden, over the fence, and I'm afraid that's the last we've seen of him. Kerry's too upset to come down and talk to you. I'm sorry.' He looked down, clearly upset. 'She's having to have a lie down.'

'Oh, I'm so sorry, too,' I said, on autopilot. I felt stupidly responsible. 'I don't know what to say …'

Mike was finishing up speaking to the police by this time. 'Yes, we're setting off home now,' he was confirming. 'About an hour. Yes, we'll wait to hear. Thanks …' he ended the call. He looked at Spencer's dad. 'No news as yet, as you probably worked out. We'll obviously let you know the minute we hear anything.' He shook his head, obviously feeling as helpless as I did about the whole sorry situation.

So did Danny Herrington, his shoulders slumped, his look defeated. And as we left the house my thoughts strayed up those stairs to where his wife was. Inebriated, maybe? Needing to keep a low profile? Or was she really hurt and upset about the day's events? I so needed to know more about Spencer's mother.

I felt devastated all the way home. What could possibly have happened to make Spencer do that? I know I'd seen evidence of a cruel streak, and anger. But what had triggered it? What had his mother said or done? I'd had long experience with kids whose mothers mistreated them. I had seen first hand how neglect, cruelty, drug abuse or just plain old chaotic parenting caused kids to develop anger that could take them off the scale. What was going on in this case? Had anything tangible gone on? Or was this just Spencer being Spencer – in which case, what was the root of his rage? If we didn't know that, how on earth could we help him?

Thank goodness he'd been fixed up with a support worker, I thought. Perhaps she could begin to tease out some answers. And she needed to, because right now I had none. I felt like I was running out of resources, and fast.

We stayed up till two in the end, waiting for a call that didn't come. Mike even called, just to check they had got the right numbers, only to be told that they were sorry, but they'd not found Spencer yet.

It was horrifying. Eight years old. I couldn't shake off the number. He was eight and he was somewhere on the streets, all alone. No nice chippy men around to help at two in the morning. Just the potential for danger at every turn. I slept only fitfully and when I did sleep I had nightmares, bookended by periods of lying awake, staring at the ceiling, imagining poor little Spencer hidden away somewhere, shivering in the cold, frightened and alone.

I must have eventually dozed off, though, because I woke with a start, hearing my alarm. It was Sunday morning, eight o'clock, and there had still been no call.

It wasn't a nightmare I'd just woken up from. It was all too real, and I was still living it.

# Chapter 14

Mike had already gone downstairs so I pulled on my dressing gown and hurried down to find out if there'd been any news. But it only took one look at his face to know there hadn't, and tears of frustration began welling in my eyes. Much as Spencer had challenged us – on so many occasions, and in so many ways – and much as he'd done things that were less than endearing, I really felt for this difficult and complicated boy, and the thought of him sleeping rough – and on our watch – really upset me. Didn't matter in the least how apparently streetwise he was. It was all wrong.

'I just wish I thought his mother even *cared*,' I sniffed, as Mike drew me in for a hug.

'Come on, love,' he said. 'I know it's worrying, but he'll be *fine*. I'm completely sure of it. Look, I've made coffee, so why don't you grab yourself one.' He paused, as if undecided about what he was about to say. 'And go and have a cigarette, if you think it'll help you. Go on. You look like you could do with one. I'll go and make another call to the police.'

Mike suggesting I have a cigarette? He must think I'm in a right state, I thought miserably, as I trudged out to the conservatory with my emergency supply. I'd been doing brilliantly – would continue to do brilliantly, I knew – but though I felt a bit guilty I also felt grateful for his under-standing. Looking out into the garden I could see that the weather was as dismal as I currently felt. It was barely light, the sky grey, the wind blowing mournfully. Altogether not a night for a young child to be sleeping rough. Not that *any* night was a night for a young child to be sleeping rough. I just prayed that Spencer had been holed up somewhere warm. I thought about when my own kids had been small. I wouldn't have let them *anywhere* near the streets at that age. Why was it that these days everything had changed so much?

I'd downed one coffee and had headed back inside to get a second cup when the doorbell went. I ran into the hall just in time to see Mike opening the door to two policemen and – praise be! – also Spencer.

I must still have been feeling more emotional than I thought, because seeing him standing there made my tears well up all over again. 'Oh, Spencer!' I cried, running to fling my arms around him. 'Oh, love, we've been frantic. Where've you *been*?'

I knelt down in the hall in my PJs and dressing gown, hugged him, kissed his cheeks and rubbed his back. I couldn't begin to describe how relieved I was to see him. All of which clearly mortified him, particularly as there was already a gaggle of small onlookers outside, keen to see why a police car had fetched up.

I let him go then, and he scurried inside, obviously keen not to have his reputation as a hard nut sullied any further, while Mike shut the door and ushered the policemen into the living room.

And it seemed that, in terms of finding Spencer, they'd had a lucky break. They'd still be looking for him, one told us, if he hadn't had the misfortune – or, more accurately, even if he didn't think so, good fortune – to try to pinch a packet of biscuits from a shopkeeper at the end of his tether.

This had happened earlier in the morning, when Spencer, by now pretty hungry, had decided to visit the corner shop near his parents in search of something he could have for breakfast. And he probably would have got away with it if it hadn't been for the fact that there was a new proprietor, who obviously didn't know Spencer, and was sick and tired of having his shop targeted by the local kids on a daily basis, and had decided he was standing for it no more.

'By all accounts,' said one of the officers, 'he physically held on to this young man from the time he called us to the time we arrived, 20 minutes later …'

'An' he slapped me, an all!' protested Spencer. 'Round the head! An' all for a measly packet of biscuits.'

'Thieving's thieving, young man,' the other officer reminded him sternly. 'Though no charges have been pressed,' he added, turning to Mike and me, 'since no harm's been done and the boy's said he's sorry. I don't think it's likely he'll be trying it again.'

I had my own thoughts about that, of course, but of much more concern to me was where he'd been and why he'd run off in the first place.

'Because I had to!' he protested. 'Because they were, like, proper kicking off.'

'Who were?' I wanted to know.

'My mum and dad. It was fine at first. An' I was being good, honest I was, Casey. Just playing in the garden with my little brother and sister. And then it kicked off. It was when they wanted to go in to get something to eat. So I'm like calling to my dad – he was by the back door, doing something to the patio, talking to Mum – an' I'm saying, "Can we have a biscuit or something?" and Coral's like, "*You* can't. You don't even live here any more." An' then she pushes me and laughs, going *na na ne na na* and all that, and I *swear* I didn't do anything …'

'And?' I asked him, conscious that he was becoming increasingly agitated.

'An' I dunno,' he said. 'Just that next thing, me mum's out in the garden, saying, "Did you hit her? Did you hit her? You hit her! Admit it." And goin' proper mental at me all of a sudden, and I'm like, "Dad saw. I didn't hit her. I never touched her."' His cheeks were red now. 'I NEVER touched her! Honest, Casey, honest, Mike. I never *ever* touched her.'

'What about your mum?' I asked, conscious that I mustn't lead him. 'What happened with your mum, then?'

He looked from one of us to the other. 'What about her? Like I said, she just went off on one, big time. Called me a load of names an' slapped me, and told me to get out of her fucking sight. I kept telling her. I kept telling her I didn't do anything to Coral. She's just my little sister, I wouldn't hurt her …'

'Your mum slapped you?' Mike asked.

'Yeah,' he said. 'Right here. Round my head. And Coral and Harvey were crying and, like, my dad was out now, and saying I should make myself scarce.' He paused and sniffed. 'So I did.' Under his blazing cheeks, he looked pale and oh-so tired.

'And so you did,' I repeated. 'Oh, Spencer …'

One of the policemen cleared his throat. 'You'll call and tell the family he's safe and sound, will you, Mrs Watson?'

I nodded. Except, in the big scheme of things, he obviously wasn't either of those things.

And it wasn't just the business of who did what to who that didn't stack up. It was the timing of the incident, as well.

'Well, I wasn't going to go back, not after that,' Spencer told us. 'Not if they were going to tell lies about me, an' that. An' I did hang around. I hung around all the bloody day, round the corner. Waiting to see your car, Mike, so I could wave you down and take me back –'

'Hang on,' I said. 'All day?'

Spencer nodded. 'Well, from whenever it was, anyway. About an hour from when you dropped me? I didn't have my watch …'

'But your father said you ran away about half an hour before we came back.'

'I never did.' He looked shocked. 'It was still the morning, definite. We'd had no lunch or anything.'

'So why on earth would he say that?'

Spencer shrugged. 'I dunno.'

'That's what young Spencer told us too,' one of the officers commented. I mentally filed it. We'd have to dig around and see what more we could find out about that one later.

'So what did you do?' I wanted to know.

'I went round me mate's,' he said. 'After I knew I must have missed you – I kept looking out, but you must have been and gone in, like, *no* time – I went round my mate Dylan's. He's safe. He knows how things are at home, so I knew he wouldn't grass me up. And his mum doesn't know I'm in care now, so I knew she wouldn't say owt. An' we asked if it was okay if I slept over at theirs because my mum and dad were going out. Dylan's mum's a bit weird,' he added sagely. 'She believes anything you tell her. So that's where I was. I stayed there till this morning.'

The expression on the faces of the policemen seemed to confirm it. They knew the area, and the people who lived there, pretty well, it seemed.

'But didn't it occur to you,' Mike asked him, 'that we would be going frantic? That your *parents* would be going frantic? Not even once?'

Spencer lowered his gaze. 'I'm really sorry, Mike, I am.' His expression changed then. 'But *they* don't care. They don't want me back. I know it. All me mum does is scream at me, and me dad doesn't stop her. What do they care that I'm off round me friend's house?'

God, I thought. Still so young, but with so much on his shoulders. Okay, so this time he'd only run as far as his friend's house. But how long would it be before he felt he had to run so far from his demons that he couldn't – and wouldn't – be found?

'Look, Spencer,' I said, once we'd been given our case number for social services and seen off the policemen. 'We all really need to sit down and think hard about all this. We need a plan, don't we? A plan that's going to work. A plan that'll stop you getting into your parents' bad books – a plan that'll help mend things with them. Okay?'

Spencer took this in. 'I know,' he said. 'But will it take long? I'm tired. Me an' Dylan played on his PlayStation all night.'

Under the circumstances, I didn't find this as amusing as I might have. I was still uncertain which version of events I should even believe. 'Okay,' I said. 'Then it's probably not the best time to do it. Tell you what, why don't you get some sleep while me and Mike sit down and think. And speak to your parents as well, because –'

'I didn't hit Coral, Casey,' he interrupted, as I said this. 'Honest to God, I didn't hit her. She's my little sister. An' I am sorry,' he said to both of us, Mike having returned from seeing out the policemen. 'Honest I am. You know, for making you worry an' that. I didn't mean to make you cry.'

And with that, he toddled off up to bed.

'So what do you think?' I asked Mike, once the house was again quiet. It wasn't even ten yet, but it felt as if we'd been up for hours.

'I don't know what to think,' he said, joining me at the kitchen table for toast and coffee. 'I mean, we know what a good liar Spencer is, don't we? And actor, come to that. But even so …'

'That's what I thought. But you know what? Both stories sound equally plausible. I mean, we know Spencer's got a temper, so what his father says is feasible … but at the same time I can visualise what Spencer's told us, too. I mean, knowing what we know about his mum already … I mean, I know it's not much, but I have a strong sense she's hanging on by her fingernails with those kids. And that she's really got it in for him. You know, taken against him. You just don't pack one of your kids off into care, do you? And what with the drinking …'

'I wonder if he's covering up for her, then?' said Mike. 'The dad. I mean, logically, if Spencer's version of events is true, then that would fit. You know, lying about when in the day the whole thing happened. If he was covering up for her, and they spent all day waiting for him to show again, then when he didn't, well, he had to lie, didn't he? Make it look as though it had only just happened …'

'I think you might be right,' I said. 'But what a thing to accuse your own son of.'

'Maybe it's an act of desperation. Maybe he felt he had no choice. I mean, given that social services are now involved with the family, it's not unreasonable to suppose that he's working on the basis that if she's found to be mistreating one or more of them she might lose them all.'

'And that would fit,' I said, 'with what Spencer told us about his mum making that deal with him. God,' I said, 'this is all looking so much grimmer than I imagined.'

'You're telling me,' Mike agreed. 'And so much more complicated. The question is, what can we *do* about it?'

# Chapter 15

It was that question, among many others, that kept my thoughts occupied for the next few days. Mike and I had decided that, for the time being at least, Spencer would need to be grounded again. Even though he'd felt he'd had no choice but to run away, he needed to learn, and fast, that this wasn't an option. Both his safety and our sanity depended on it. I made a mental note to speak to his new support worker, Penny, in the hopes that this would be something she'd cover in her first session with him, and hopefully arm him with some alternative courses of action when he felt unable to face the world and its problems. I also decided that I would once again voice our suspicions about Kerry's drinking to both John and Glenn. I had mentioned it before but, as it was only guesswork, the matter had been glossed over and not really discussed.

'But Casey, it wasn't *my* fault,' Spencer had argued when I told him after school the following Monday that he would be grounded. 'What else could I do? Stay there and get a hiding for doing nothing?'

'I know that's how it must look to you,' I tried to explain. 'But this is exactly what we talked about last week, wasn't it? I made it quite clear that we had to work on all this running away malarkey; that we needed to look at other ways. And what about calling us? That was the drill. That you'd go to a phone box and *call* us. You scared me and Mike half to death, we were so worried about you.'

And we had been through it with him pretty comprehensively. There had recently been a run of adverts on the television encouraging young people to use a new 'reverse charge' service from public phones. As it used letters rather than numbers, spelling out R-E-V-E-R-S-E on the key pad, it was easily accessible to even younger children. Spencer had picked up on it straight away and we'd drilled it in to him that in urgent circumstances this is what he would have to do.

Spencer's face was a picture of incomprehension. 'I know, Casey, but I forgot all about going to the phone box. I've hardly even seen any phone boxes, either.'

I made another mental note, to familiarise myself with where all the public phone boxes were these days. That was another worry – soon to become an even bigger one. Public phone boxes were disappearing at an incredible rate of knots. Another thing I should sit down and go through with Spencer, who was too young to own a mobile phone, was the alternative, of asking someone in a responsible position to make a call for him – a shopkeeper, a park warden, a lollipop lady. Not that any of those options would be readily available to a child wandering the streets late at night.

Spencer didn't really understand the whole concept of people fretting about him anyway. That was all too clear. 'But why were you worried?' he asked again. 'You know I can look after myself.'

'Love, that's the whole point. You're eight years old. You shouldn't be having to look after yourself. Spencer, love, other kids your age don't do things like this. They let adults take care of them. That's how it's supposed to be. Once you're an adult, then of course you'd want to look after yourself. But not now.' He still looked unconvinced. It really did seem completely alien to him, the concept that anyone might be worried about his welfare. Which made me wonder. For just how long and how often had this little boy been left to roam the streets? 'Spencer,' I tried again. 'Yes, you might be able to handle yourself for a night or two, all being well. But is that what you want? Sleeping in bins? Thieving to get food? Being cold and lonely? That's no life, is it?'

Once again I could see how strongly he felt the injustice. 'Better than getting a beating,' he said defiantly.

'Well, that's as maybe,' I said. 'But while you're with us these are the rules, and a few nights indoors aren't going to kill you.'

I might as well have been talking in Swahili.

For all that it wouldn't kill him, Spencer made it clear that being made to stay in – properly stay in, as opposed to pretending to stay in and absconding out of his bedroom window – was a major challenge. As we'd already noticed, he was an intelligent, energetic child, and keeping him occupied after school each day was beginning to feel like a full-time job. He would prowl around the house, dash up and down the stairs for no apparent reason, stare mournfully out of the window and endlessly moan, while engaged in an activity, about how bored he was going to be when he'd finished it, and how boring the next one would probably be too. Thinking about his mother, and the houseful of children and the probable drink problems, I wondered if she just grew sick of the sound of his endless moaning and flouncing and demanding, and had come to adopt an out of sight, out of mind policy very early on.

But it wasn't my job to do that, or even an option. And it wasn't right, either. Children didn't ask to be born, did they? So we baked cakes, made Airfix models and built extravagant creations out of Lego, the only respite from the relentless round of keeping him entertained being when Riley dropped by with Levi and Jackson.

Having the little ones to play with was one thing that did help, and when Riley arrived for tea towards the end of the week we could enjoy a quiet 20 minutes in the kitchen while Spencer, in the conservatory, set about making them cars out of Duplo, which he told them they could then use for a monster crash derby, in which they could smash them all to pieces again.

The little ones, like many a small boy before them, found this whole idea tremendously exciting. They both giggled excitedly, having readily been caught up in Spencer's enthusiastic appetite for destruction.

'He must miss his siblings,' Riley said to me, as we went into the kitchen to grab a coffee each. 'Must be hard for him, coming from such a big family, to try and keep himself amused.' She popped her head around the conservatory door. 'Hey, Spence, don't get them over-excited,' she warned him. 'We're off swimming in a bit, and I don't want them hyper.'

'I won't,' Spencer promised, upending the tub of bricks onto the floor. He grinned up at her. 'Can I come?' he said. 'I love swimming. An' I'm good, too. I could help you.'

Riley glanced across at me. I could tell what she was thinking: that losing Spencer at a swimming pool would be no kind of fun. 'Sorry, not tonight,' I said. 'Remember, you're still grounded.'

'But maybe next time?' He looked suddenly animated. 'When you next go? I'm good, I am, honest. Swim like a fish, I do. It's because I take after my mum.'

'Your mum?' Riley asked. 'Is she a good swimmer then?'

'Yeah, she was a champion,' he said proudly. 'She got trophies and stifficates and medals too. They're all at ours.'

'Really?' I said, trying to square the image of the woman that I knew with the idea of a young sporting star. It was hard.

'Yeah,' said Spencer. 'When she was young and that, anyway. She used to take me swimming lots when I was little, but not now.'

'Why?' Riley asked.

'Because she don't ever do anything with me no more.' He started clicking bricks together, mechanically, as if in thought.

'So how far can you swim, then?' I asked, keen to change the mood.

'I done my six hundred metres,' he said, obviously keen to change it too. 'I would've have done my thousand metres too, last year, at school. But they stopped us going in my year, cos there's not enough kids for them to pay for the bus.'

'That's a shame,' I said, and as I did so I had a small eureka moment. *I* should take him swimming. No, it absolutely wasn't my favourite activity, which was probably why it hadn't crossed my mind up to now. But it would be perfect. Something energetic, that would tire him out, plus a precious positive link to his mother – a chance, even if it would only be in spirit, for him to bond with the mother who'd given birth to him, who'd presumably, in the early days, cherished him, but who now seemed to find him so hard to get along with.

'You know what, Spencer?' I lied. 'I love swimming too. How about you and I go together after school tomorrow? It doesn't break the rule about grounding if I take you.'

'Mum,' said Riley, 'why don't you just come with us today?'

So that was that, and there was no backing down. Time to dredge out my old costume.

True to his word, Spencer turned out to be an excellent swimmer. He could dive superbly too, and also swim almost a length under water – no mean feat for a child of his young age. He had a wonderful crawl, which looked as if it was completely second nature, and really did seem to have genuine talent. Would this be the key, I wondered, that would unlock the door into his psyche? Enthused and encouraged, I vowed that afternoon that swimming would become a regular thing on the calendar, for as long as we had him, and that I'd make enquiries about opportunities to get him some professional coaching, and maybe see about him joining the leisure-centre swimming club. I felt really excited about it. It was like I'd suddenly found a key that just might unlock some secret part of this strange little runaway boy.

I also marvelled, that night, while Spencer enthused to Mike about his swimming, at the thought of his mum being so athletic in her younger days. I wondered how life had turned so terribly negative for her to be at such a bad place that she couldn't even function sufficiently to care for the middle of her five children. What was it with Spencer's family? I simply couldn't fathom it.

And if I felt a pang of sadness about Kerry, I felt it even more for Danny. Spencer's dad seemed to be doing his level best to keep things together; how hard must it be for him to see the current version of the presumably driven, sporty girl he had married.

But there was little I could do about the Herrington family – my role was to try and help Spencer, who I was pleased to see responded really well to his new hobby. It seemed to deal brilliantly with his excess energy, and his mood improved immeasurably, and as October gave way to November we were going three times a week, days on which, once home, he needed nothing more than bath and bed – just as my own kids had done at his age. Just as kids did everywhere, in fact, which really felt like progress. Not that I'd get in and swim with him every time. I'd go in with him on week nights, when the pool was fairly quiet, but on Saturdays, when the place teemed with over-excited youngsters, I decided I'd leave him to it, grabbing a coffee and sitting as a spectator at the pool edge, in the little café that was adjacent.

But my confidence in the merits of Spencer's positive new hobby was about to be thrown into as much turmoil as the wave machine created. And once again, it left me shaken and confused.

It was our second Saturday and, Spencer having been in the pool around half an hour, I decided I'd leave my table and grab myself a second coffee, to warm me up. Winter was really setting in now and, despite the heating, I found I was quickly getting chilly, sitting at the edge of the café, doing nothing. I glanced over before I did so to see Spencer playing happily. He made friends quickly and easily, and here was no exception – he was playing with a group and they were involved in some sort of game that involved swimming underwater and doing handstands. I waited until he spotted me and mimed what I was doing, upon which he waved and did a thumbs up.

My coffee dispensed, I then returned, and naturally looked for Spencer, but could no longer see him among the group of kids. Putting my coffee down, I then patrolled the row of tables at the pool side, and, still failing to locate him, felt the first stirrings of anxiety. It wasn't fear, exactly – I knew he was safe in the water – just the uncomfortable feeling that something wasn't right.

With still no sign of him, I decided I needed to trust my instincts. I abandoned both my coffee and the café, and made my way to the spectator area on the other side of the pool. Over here was the play pool for the toddlers and babies. It wasn't a place I'd expect to see him, as he preferred the deep water, but, even so, that's where I found him.

He waved and grinned as he saw me, but even as he did so the uncomfortable feeling in my stomach persisted. There was something about the scene that wasn't right.

I waved back, still uneasy, trying to put my finger on it, trying to work out what it was about the scene that felt wrong. And then I saw it. Two small legs suddenly emerged from the water, kicking out, feet up, at Spencer's side. Before I could catch my breath what was wrong became obvious as, before my eyes, Spencer, still smiling angeli-cally at me, calmly pulled a small girl's head out of the water by her pony tail. Worse than that, he'd obviously been holding her under, for as she righted herself, coming up, gasping for air, she lunged right at him, screaming and crying. I watched stupefied as Spencer, deflecting her blows, then pulled her calmly out of the water onto the tiled edge.

Since I was not allowed onto the pool edge, and Spencer was still smiling at me, I furiously beckoned him over. Having crossed the small pool, and then the deep end, which he knifed through expertly, he emerged and, still grinning, looked enquiringly at me. 'Is it time to get out?' he asked innocently. I shuddered involuntarily. Just at that moment his demeanour scared me.

I was almost speechless. 'Spencer,' I hissed. 'What were you *doing* with that young girl?'

'What girl?' He looked around quizzically.

'The one you were holding under the water,' I answered. 'Spencer, you know full well which girl!'

'Oh, you mean Molly?' he answered. 'She's okay, we were just playing. I had to count how long she could stay under water.'

'No, Spencer,' I said, 'that was *not* what was happening. She was scared and she was panicking. You were *holding* her down.'

Spencer's expression altered then. Only subtly, but enough to confirm that I'd been right in what I'd seen. He'd thought he'd got away with it, and now he'd been rumbled. He looked petulant. Defiant. And cross.

'I'm off to get dressed,' he huffed. 'An' I'm not coming swimming with you again. You're just like my mum,' he said. 'Always accusing me of stuff.' And with that, he stormed off to the changing rooms.

I was left feeling sick and confused. There was no way on earth I could trust him to go swimming again on his own. But what should I think? What should I do? I knew what I'd seen, and it chilled me. He'd deliberately tried to hurt that little girl – he could have even drowned her. Yet to him, I mused, as we drove home in a mutual stony silence, it was all part of a game. And in the face of his insistence on that point, what *could* I do? Was this a deeper insight into the sort of child his parents were dealing with? A child with no understanding of causing pain to other children? A child who didn't care who he hurt? I thought back to all the other instances of cruelty in Spencer, and to the few insights I'd gleaned into the behaviour of his parents. What was the cause and what was the effect here? I realised I honestly didn't have the first clue.

Thank goodness the support worker had a background in psychology. As for me, I decided, sadly, my little halcyon patch had ended. I was shocked, I was upset and I was baffled.

# Chapter 16

It was frustrating, though perhaps inevitable, that the first thing Spencer's new support worker suggested when she turned up for our initial meeting was that her preferred activity to do with him was to take him swimming. It would, she commented, be so good for him.

Inevitable precisely because it *had* been so good for him. And, as a consequence, my reports – which I would log and email daily – had been equally positive in tone. Not that she took a whole lot of notice of my fears. Even after I'd explained in detail what I'd witnessed the previous Saturday, and how hard it would be to supervise him properly, her response was to look at me with an un-fazed expression and tell me I really shouldn't worry.

'He'd have to be pretty damned fast to escape me,' she said cheerfully. 'Don't you worry. I'll obviously keep a very close eye. No, it's clear swimming's something that's thera-peutic for Spencer. And in terms of how I bond with him, that's important. I'll be able to get to know him so much better if we have our interactions in an environment he feels comfortable with.'

Even if it compromises other children's safety? I wondered, though not out loud, as it was patently pointless. I'd told her what had happened, and it clearly didn't bother her. And who was I to judge anyway? She had a wealth of experience. Perhaps she knew what she was doing a whole lot better than it might seem. Or perhaps not.

'Oh, and I've been speaking to Glenn, too,' she said. 'We've had a long discussion and we both feel that if we're going to make progress with his problems, then Spencer needs to be allowed a bit more freedom.'

'Really?' I began.

She nodded. 'So, ideally, we want you, if you feel you could, of course', she added sweetly, 'to look into alternatives to grounding him, basically.'

I digested this carefully. It took me all of half a second. 'But it's him having freedom that's *causing* all the problems,' I answered. I was getting really rather irritated by now. Did she know anything about the child she was taking on? At all? Or had she just decided – Glenn, too – that I was making things out to be worse than they actually were? 'Grounding him,' I persisted, 'has been the only punishment – strategy, whatever – that has *worked*. Nothing else, in terms of sanctions, really bothers him.'

Penny's expression softened. And in a way that made mine harden somewhat. I could see I might be about to receive a small lecture. And I was. 'The thing is, Casey, and I don't want to offend you, is that this programme is not about punishment at all. The only time, as you know, when kids can't have their home comforts – and, as you know, that includes peer time – is when they haven't earned enough points to "buy" them. If we veer away from that formula, then we miss the whole point of the programme – a programme that we both know has been shown to work, and work well.'

So that was me told. And despite my brain telling my face not to, it blushed. I was being told off, and it didn't feel nice at all. And what made matters worse was that I knew Penny was, in one respect, anyway, quite right. What she had just said was exactly what Mike and I had been taught, back in training. For me to ground Spencer was effectively not only punishing him, but punishing him twice, because it was ignoring the points he'd already earned – and on a programme that, as Penny pointed out, wasn't based around punishment, for a zillion reasons, all of which I already knew.

No, I had to admit to myself that I *had* veered from the programme. That I was treating Spencer as I would have treated my own children – normal, well-adjusted children, without deep-rooted psychological problems, apart from Kieron, of course, who had a mild form of Asperger's. Children for whom straightforward punishments like groundings normally had the desired effect. But Spencer was none of those things, obviously. And I knew I was grounding him for pragmatic rather than therapeutic reasons. To keep him safe, yes, but not as a means to help him negotiate his emotional issues. All of which might have sounded like so much psycho-jargon, but was right, for all that. I felt chastened, and not least because of the fact that it was Spencer himself who had also pointed out some of these facts to me some weeks ago, when he was trying to work out how he could manipulate the system. I remembered him using the exact words, in fact: 'That's like punishing me twice.'

'I do understand,' I admitted. 'It's just that when you're the one dealing with these things day to day, it's sometimes hard to see the wood for the trees. I guess I'll just have to take things right back to basics. What kinds of extra freedom did you have in mind?'

Penny looked happier now she'd imparted her wisdoms. 'Well,' she said, 'it's important that Spencer sees himself as having the same opportunities as every other child. The main thing he needs to work on is accepting boundaries.'

*You don't say*, I couldn't help but think. But I kept my mouth clamped tight shut. 'We need him to be allowed to play out for, say, an hour a day, so that when he does misbehave he has to pay for it with points. D'you see? If he's out, he has the means to *lose* points, which will make him appreciate the relationship between points and privileges … i.e. learn about consequences. If he's out, you see, and taking responsibility for his behaviour, then the onus is firmly on *him* to behave. Grounded, he learns nothing. D'you see?' I kept my mouth shut again, difficult though it was. It wasn't easy, having spelt out what I already knew, even if, temporarily, I seemed to have forgotten it. 'I suppose it's really a case,' she finished, 'of giving him enough rope to hang himself with. If you want to look at it that way, anyway. But if we're consistent, as you know, then eventually he'll recognise that he has that precious thing – autonomy. Autonomy to allow himself to live a happy life.'

She didn't say 'D'you see?' this time, for which I was grateful. But she was right. That was exactly what he needed to be able to do. But at the same time I refused to beat myself up too much. Before Spencer had come to live with us, if I'd heard anyone else complaining about how difficult it was to control an eight-year-old, I suppose I would have found it a bit hard to believe, too. And, like Penny, I might have come across as a little patronising.

'You're quite right,' I said. 'And I'm absolutely willing to play it by the book. I just need to know that the support's there if I need it, and that if it all goes wrong we can look at our strategy again.'

'Oh course,' she gushed now. 'Casey, that goes without saying. We're also arranging for Spencer to go and see a clinical psychologist – did Glenn mention it? Might as well start as we mean to go on, and find out exactly what we're dealing with. And, look, I know this is new territory – every child is new territory, aren't they? – and having read what I've read, I know you and Mike really have your work cut out with Spencer. But you can trust me, I won't do anything half-heartedly, I promise. I'm on this 100 per cent, and I *really* want to make a difference.'

Penny looked so sincere now that I felt guilty about my misgivings. She was obviously experienced and obviously committed, and I felt confident that she meant every single word she said. I apologised for seeming so doubtful initially, which she gracefully shrugged off with a laugh.

'I can seem something of the zealot, I know,' she admitted. 'So don't worry. I'm used to it. And I can't wait to meet Spencer. I'll be around after school on Thursday, so if you could perhaps have his swimming things ready? And then I'll take him for a burger, so don't worry about his tea.' She winked conspiratorially. 'I always find kids seem to open up brilliantly when shovelling junk food down their necks, don't you?'

I grinned back. Something we finally had in common. Now she was speaking *my* language.

The promise of meeting Penny, and of the resumption of his swimming sessions, seemed to be enough to keep Spencer happy and well-behaved for several days. He was also thrilled to be allowed back out to play on the street, and seemed determined to work hard to maintain his points so that it wasn't a privilege once again denied him. That said, I'd been careful to tighten up his targets, and ensure there were no loopholes with which to try and catch me out.

And the Thursday itself was a good day. In the morning came the letter containing the appointment with the psychologist, and the promise of perhaps finding out what really made Spencer tick, and in the afternoon came Penny, and an equal amount of promise. Just seeing her with Spencer gave me a real boost of hope.

She was obviously a natural – one of those rare people who seemed to click with children without trying – and right away I could tell this relationship would be a real positive in Spencer's life. 'Go on, you little scamp,' she told him playfully. 'I've already heard all about you and your swimming. Think you can beat me in a race, do you? Bet you don't.'

'Bet I do!' Spencer cried, gleefully. 'I'm like a fish, me. Just ask Casey.'

'You are, love,' I agreed. 'Now go and grab your bag. It's in the conservatory. This is Penny, by the way ...'

But I might as well have been talking to myself, and soon was. Within seconds, it seemed, the two of them were out of the door. Two hours, she'd told me. Two hours and a promise that by the time she brought him home he'd be way too tired for wanting to go out or run me ragged. So, I thought happily, Thursdays would be good days from now on. And I was right to be confident. They were.

Saturdays too, it turned out. At least the next couple of Saturdays. Because Penny had decided that to form a strong bond with Spencer she'd take him swimming and for lunch, too, plus, having consulted with me, give him the treat of an ice cream at Giorgio's, a place in town we'd introduced him to, and which he loved. And I agreed with her thinking – any positive adult intervention in his life could only be a good thing. Plus the more consistent Spencer's routine, the better it would be for him.

And good for me, as well, to have a Saturday to myself, of which I took full advantage (sadly, for Mike, he was busy working) by spending the day with Riley and David and the little ones, with Kieron and Lauren joining us for lunch. Spencer had been with us for almost four months now, I realised, and, bar the disastrous stint of respite, this was the first time since then that I'd been able to enjoy the simple pleasure of seeing my family without the worry of what my foster child was getting up to. It was a glorious, invigorating few hours.

I was feeling similarly positive about the appointment with the psychologist, as, rather endearingly, was Spencer himself, who declared himself intrigued and just a little bit excited at the prospect of someone 'getting to know' his brain.

He'd been well prepared by Penny about what would be happening and why, and when we arrived you'd have thought it was Disneyland we were visiting, rather than having an appointment with a shrink.

But when they came out – after I'd spent half an hour or so catching up with my gossip mags in the waiting room – I couldn't help but notice that Spencer looked disappointed.

'Was it okay, love?' I asked him, once our goodbyes had been done and we'd set off for home in the car.

'It was okay,' he said, sounding deflated. 'I guess. But it wasn't what I 'spected. Penny said it would be all about me, but all he seemed to want to know about was my family.'

'Really, love?' I said. 'But perhaps that's how it works. He gets to know you a bit by hearing about where you come from. Perhaps it'll be more about you when you next go.'

'Yeah, maybe,' he said. Though he didn't look convinced. 'But how's he gonna work out anything that'll teach him about my brain, when all he wants to know is 'bout my brothers 'n' sisters?'

I smiled at him through the rear-view mirror. He really was such a little thinker, and this had clearly foxed him. 'I don't know, love,' I answered honestly, 'but psychologists are very clever people. I'm sure he knows what he's doing. I'll bet he's planning on getting to know that big old brain of yours next week. Bet he can't wait. Hey, now, Mr Long-face. How about some Chipmunks?'

The workings of Spencer's brain might have still been a mystery to the psychologist, but some things were set in stone. I didn't have to wait to hear the answer.

It would be another two appointments, and a further week of waiting, before we got to hear about what the psychologist thought of Spencer and his brain. The psychologist himself called me, while Spencer was at school, to run through the main points that the interviews had thrown up, which he said he'd also send out in a letter.

And just as well, because, as with anything complex and medical, I couldn't take it all in at once.

'Basically,' he said, wasting no time on preamble, 'my opinion, based on the few sessions I've had with him, is that young Spencer, if clinically assessed and diagnosed, would in all likelihood be diagnosed as a sociopath.'

I took this in, slowly, feeling a stirring of disquiet. It was a word I knew well. It was a word with clear negative associations. Not a psychopath, thank God, but still ... 'So what,' I asked, 'are the actual implications for Spencer?'

The psychologist explained that, essentially, if his opinion was correct, Spencer's brain wasn't wired like other kids' were. Though Spencer appeared to display a range of normal emotions, such as pleasure, affection, joy and sadness and so on, he didn't *feel* them – at least, not like other children did. 'All he's done,' the psychologist said, 'is to master the art of mimicking them. Doing the things he's seen others do to make it *look* as if he feels them when, in reality, he does no such thing.'

'So what do we do now?' I said, as the implication of this began to hit me. 'You know, to help him? What sort of thing should we be doing?'

'Well, I'd certainly suggest behavioural therapy might be helpful. Cognitive behavioural therapy. With help, Spencer might be able to be taught how to adjust some of his less acceptable behaviours, and, of course, continuing work with a therapist might be helpful, to assist him in learning to have empathy with others, and to be able to understand how others think and act. But it's all in my letter, and I'll obviously be in touch with social services …'

And that, to all intents and purposes, was that. Spencer was what he was. End of. And the 'what' was so depressing. 'I can't take it in,' I told Mike, as we lay in bed that evening, remembering all the 'mights' the psychologist had used. 'Might' be helpful. 'Might' be useful. 'He can be so *loving*. So genuinely loving and affectionate. I can't get my head round the idea that he's just acting it all.'

Mike frowned. 'But we've also seen the other side of him, don't forget – the violence, the cruelty, the pleasure in causing pain. Except, if what you say is true, it's not even about pleasure, is it? Just that he doesn't even register that other people *feel* pain. So,' he said, reaching to switch off his bedside light, 'what's the plan, then?'

'That's just it,' I said. 'There isn't one. Not really. I mean, they'll presumably keep up the support work and so on, and, budget permitting, I suppose they might book him for some of this behavioural therapy. But, no, that's the last thing I asked the psychologist about. How to make him better.'

'And?'

'And as I said, that's it. They *can't* make him better. *We* can't make him better, Mike. He apparently is what he is. A sociopath. There *isn't* any cure.'

# Chapter 17

It was a damning diagnosis for anyone to receive, obviously, but for a shunned eight-year-old boy with the world on his shoulders it felt the cruellest of fates I could imagine. What would happen to him now, if there was no hope of a cure? As Spencer's wasn't a court-ordered placement, i.e. one in which the court could act autonomously, this would all need to be discussed with his parents. Was there any chance, having already labelled him so unmanageable, that they would have him back when they read the report?

I didn't think so, but during the days following the call from the psychologist it was as if Spencer knew all about how he'd been labelled and was determined to prove it wasn't true. Nonsense, I knew – he had no idea about any of it – but at every turn, it seemed, he'd provide a new example to prove he wasn't the unfeeling automaton he'd been described as.

'Look at him,' I whispered to Mike, as we stood and watched the local Guy Fawkes Night fireworks a couple of days later. They were being held at Kieron's football club and the whole family had come to watch. Mike followed my gaze, to where Spencer, just in front of us, was crouched by Jackson's buggy, one hand holding tight onto Levi's as they watched, and whispering calming words to his slightly frightened baby brother. 'Don't be scared,' he was saying, 'it's only the bangs the pretty lights make. They won't hurt you.'

Mike and I exchanged glances. How, we agreed sadly, could something like that be manufactured? If Spencer was a sociopath, how could he spontaneously display such loving behaviour towards the little ones? It didn't make any kind of sense to either of us.

And if I'd been knocked a bit sideways by the latest shift in Spencer's fortunes, the next home visit – which I suspected wouldn't help things – was another thing looming uncomfortably. Though Spencer, once again, was all excited anticipation. 'It won't be long now, I bet,' he said, as we discussed it one evening. 'Till I'm fixed and can go home. I seen that brain doctor for lots of times now, haven't I? An' he's good at his job. Penny said so.'

He was sitting beside me on the sofa. Close enough to touch, but not touching. I reached out to squeeze his hand, and he immediately snuggled up to me. 'Fixed, love?' I asked, keen to probe gently. 'So what's he fixing?'

I felt him shrug. 'I dunno, really. It's just what my mum said. She said I can't come home till I'm fixed. That's what he's doing, isn't it?' He tipped his head to look up at me. 'That's what she means, isn't it? That he needs to get me fixed. So I can be like the others, and go home for good.'

I felt a lump swell in my throat as I tousled his hair. If only life could be that simple. If only children didn't see things in such damning black and white. He was broken, and his mum didn't want him till he was mended. No! It went against every natural law of parental love. No wonder he had problems with empathy. I pulled him closer still and cuddled him tightly. 'You know, babes,' I said, 'it's a little difficult to explain, but you know, I am *sure* your mum loves you, "fixed" or otherwise. She's a mum and that's what mums mostly do. Her putting you into care' – I noticed he didn't pull me up on that fact now – 'was, well, her reaching out for help, because she couldn't cope.'

I felt Spencer slowly shake his head against my chest. 'She sometimes loves me, Casey. *Sometimes* she does. But not *all* the time. Sometimes she hates me. An' when she hates me she really hates me. She calls me the devil's prawn.'

'The what?' I asked, unsure I'd correctly heard what he'd said.

'The devil's prawn,' he repeated. 'An' that's not good, is it?'

I shook my head. 'No,' I said, trying to swallow the lump away as I did so. 'No, sweetheart. You're right. That's not so good.'

But for all Spencer's quiet unhappiness about his mother, he was a child, and like all children he kept trying to adapt to his circumstances, building himself up, as the days passed and the next home visit drew nearer, with increasingly unrealistic expectations. It was as if the previous visits had never even happened – or, if they had, that they'd morphed into completely different animals; all fun and frolics with his family, where happiness reigned supreme. No running off, no altercations, no being brought back by the police.

'I wonder if Dad'll take me fishing?' he mused, the evening before the visit, when we'd all sat down to plates of stew and dumplings. 'He did once, you know. When I was little. I loved it.' He chewed thoughtfully on his tea for a moment. 'But he had to stop taking me.'

'Why's that?' Mike asked.

'Because I'm his favourite,' Spencer answered. 'But that's not fair on the others, really, is it?'

'Having a favourite child isn't, no,' I agreed, curious to know what he was driving at. 'But why did that mean he had to stop taking you fishing?'

Spencer swallowed another mouthful before he answered.

'Because he had to act bad,' he said, seeming to think carefully about his words. 'You know, act bad to me so's the others didn't get jealous. Cos that wouldn't be fair, would it?' He looked at us in turn, seeming anxious that we understood, that we agreed.

'Act bad?' I prompted. What did he mean by those words?

'You know, make like I wasn't his favourite,' he continued. 'Pretend he didn't like me.'

'Did he say that?'

Spencer nodded. 'Yeah, kind of. Like he has to do with Mum.'

Curiouser and curiouser. 'With Mum?'

He nodded. 'Like, he has to pretend I'm not his favourite, so that she doesn't get jealous as well.'

He rolled his eyes, as if world weary but accepting of this oddity, and continued to scoop up his stew. But the only things I could digest now were his words – well, try to; they were making no kind of sense to me.

'I'm not sure I understand what you mean, love,' I ventured. 'Is that what you think? That your mum doesn't like your dad loving you?'

Spencer stopped eating and shrugged. 'Prob'ly. But I don't care if she hates me sometimes, because I hate her too. But, you know?' He paused. 'You know, I wish sometimes she *did* love me, cos then it would teach her a lesson. Cos she'd be upset, wouldn't she? If she knew I didn't like her. Or did something bad, an' that, wouldn't she?'

'Sweetheart,' I said. 'I'm sure you're wrong about your mum. I think she does love you. I think she loves you a lot. She just doesn't know how to show it. Not properly, that's all.' I put my cutlery down. 'Hey, you know when we were talking the other day, and you were telling me how she said you needed to be fixed?'

Spencer nodded, his mouth full of dumpling. 'Hmm-mm.'

'Well, you know, sometimes it's not the kids who need fixing. It's the grown-ups. Sometimes it's the mums and dads who are the ones who need fixing and when children go into care – like *you* have, to stay with us – that's why they have social workers go to visit them. They go there to help them work out all the grown-up things that need fixing. They need help, just like you do. Okay?'

'So that's what's happening, then, is it? My mum and dad are being fixed, too?'

'I really hope so,' I said. 'We both do, don't we, Mike?'

God, I thought. If only I believed that.

Spencer's comments about his family, muddled and compli-cated as they were, actually helped crystallise my own thinking. Neither Mike nor I could really make sense of what he'd said about his dad – I doubted Spencer himself could really make sense of that relationship – as, given what we'd seen of the man, it seemed odd. Was Spencer intimat-ing that he was mean to him too? It all felt really weird. But one thing was a constant I knew to be true. Long experi-ence with damaged kids had shown me time and time again that if a child is told enough times that they are bad, or that they're evil, they will – almost inevitably – come to believe it. If 'devil's spawn' was Spencer's mother's expression of choice – *God*, I thought, *how could she?* – then I could only be thankful that he didn't have an adult sense of what it meant.

I also thought back to what the psychologist has said, in his report, about Spencer seeming to lack a 'moral centre'. Was that such a surprise, really? Given the dysfunctional parenting he'd experienced? Children developed a sense of morality from whoever was raising them. But how were you supposed to develop morality when you were being parented so poorly? So haphazardly? With a dad who 'acts bad' to you to create the idea that you are anything but his favour-ite, and a mother who apparently both loved and hated you and told you that you were the spawn of the devil?

It was clearly an incredibly complex situation but, unprofessional though it might have been, my feelings were simple. I felt like screaming at the pair of them, shaking some sense into them – particularly Kerry. YOU'VE DONE THIS! Can't you see? Done SO much damage!

And it was an impression that was only endorsed the following morning, when we arrived at the Herringtons' at 9.30, as planned, to find Spencer's mother staring at us, stony faced, on the doorstep, her arms folded across her chest, her expression petulant.

Not that this was entirely unexpected. John Fulshaw had called the previous evening, after Spencer was in bed, to let us know that social services had been to visit the family and given the Herringtons something of a dressing down.

This wasn't the whimsical, gentle 'fixing' I'd alluded to with Spencer. Far from it. It had been made clear that when he was with them he would be their responsibility, that it was unacceptable for him to be allowed out to roam the streets, and that, accordingly, they must make an effort to occupy him. It sounded crazy, put like that – they were the parents, not naughty children – and also pointless, since they seemed in no rush to have him back, so perhaps they weren't that motivated anyway. But the key thing, as ever, was that they were now in the system. And Spencer was not their only vulnerable child.

Kerry's expression seemed clear. She wasn't happy.

'As if I don't have enough to contend with,' she moaned, as soon as we were within shouting distance. 'Without having this little bastard under my feet all day! I presume, as he can't go out, you'll be picking him up earlier?'

I was open-mouthed. Spencer could hear every word. As could her husband, who was standing just behind her. As well he might be. It was obvious to all of us that she was slurring her words and, as we got level, you could smell the drink easily. She was seriously drunk. It was obvious.

'Spencer, I –' he began, but Spencer didn't allow him to finish. His face first crumpling, and then hardening into a scowl, he pushed through the open doorway past his parents.

'Shut your gob!' he yelled at her. 'You're just a bitch!' He was crying hard as he disappeared inside.

'I am so sorry,' Spencer's dad said, obviously embarrassed. 'You two go. It'll be okay. Spencer will be fine when he calms down.' Kerry had by now turned and lurched off herself, but he still checked behind him before leaning out and whispering conspiratorially, 'I'll have a word with her. I'm so sorry you had to hear all that.'

Sorry *we* had to? What about Spencer?

Mike gave Danny a tight grin. 'Don't worry about it, mate. I'm sure you'll handle things okay. See you at four …'

'And maybe your son as well, this time,' he finished, out of Danny's earshot, as we climbed back into the car.

And, unprecedented as it was, this time we did see him at four. We'd had another day wandering around the shops in the nearby village, and this time, with so much on our minds about the future, it had felt a pretty long time, as well. With the psychologist's opinion about Spencer's future chances looming large, we couldn't help but think the worst: were his parents *really* likely to have him back?

And looking at the state of his mother that morning, were social services even likely to let them? And could *we* just let this go, for that matter? Spencer's mother wasn't fit to look after herself, let alone her children. Shouldn't something be done?

It was in a negative frame of mind, then, that we duly turned up again in Spencer's street, and we were therefore surprised to see him on the doorstep, with his mum's hand on his shoulder, and looking – dare we even think it? – calm and happy.

As we pulled up, he waved and started down the path to the car. No point in us getting out then, I thought as we watched him, a thought confirmed when, with a small wave, Kerry turned and went inside. She too looked less agitated, from what we could see at this distance. Clearly keen to be shot of him – how long had they been standing there, waiting? – but then Rome, I thought grimly, wasn't built in a day.

But no sooner had Spencer got to the car than he signalled to Mike to wind his window down.

'I've just remembered,' he said, 'I forgot my present. Won't be a sec.'

He ran back up the front path and then around the side of the house, and for a moment I panicked, thinking it had been too good to be true, and that what he was actually doing was running away again. But no sooner had I started to open my car door than he was back again, carrying a box under his arm.

'It's my dinosaur books. All of them,' he announced proudly as he clambered in. 'An' I'm going to put them away somewhere very, very safe, so Levi and Jackson can't get at them with all their crayons an' stuff.'

We both laughed at this, Mike letting out an audible sigh – relieved as I was that the day had worked out. I laughed again as Spencer then leaned forward between us and cheekily ordered that we listen to the Chipmunks on the journey home. 'An' I expect both of you,' he commanded, 'to sing along.'

We duly obliged and the trip seemed to pass in a flash, and when we got indoors I think all of our moods were much lighter than they'd been in a very long time. And it was a mood that continued right up till Spencer's bedtime – one that was earlier than usual for a Saturday evening, because the day had clearly tired him right out.

But in a good way. 'Hey, love,' I said, as I tucked him in and kissed him. 'Mike and I are really proud of you for today.'

He smiled sleepily. 'It was a good day,' he said decisively, his arms round my neck. 'See, I'm not the devil's prawn, am I, Casey?'

I hugged him tight, squeezing the breath out of him, almost. 'Not even the devil's chipmunk,' I said.

Back downstairs, curled on the sofa with the latest instalment of *American Idol*, I allowed my mind to drift to the strange nature of what we did. How Mike and I, as foster carers, routinely brushed up against lives and families so much more complex than our own, but without any real sense of how they functioned. What went on in Spencer's family, we'd probably *never* really know. It wasn't our place to. As with all the kids who came to us – from other foster homes, children's homes or, in this unusual case, the family home – our job was just to care for Spencer while the authorities made decisions about how best to manage his future. Was there a slim chance he might be returned home eventually? Or, if not quite home, then at least to some semblance of a happy life? Was there any hope that whatever demons were responsible for this desperate situation might be laid to rest sufficiently for that to happen?

Yes, the odds were long, and I was too much the realist to believe in miracles, but maybe they'd just got a little shorter.

# Chapter 18

My positive mood carried right on through the rest of the weekend, bobbing along in the wake of Spencer's continued good behaviour and the sense that at last there'd been a positive home visit. Not perfect – I still had so many misgivings about Spencer's mother and the state we had seen her in that morning – but at least evidence that progress could be made. If nothing else, it seemed clear Spencer's dad wanted to hold things together, however hard a job that might be.

We spent almost all of Sunday round at Riley and David's, following up a long, long winter walk with a fabulous roast dinner, made all the better by the fact that I hadn't had to cook it. A perfect family day in every way.

And it was clear I wasn't the only one with a spring in my step going into the next week. When I dropped Spencer off at school on the following frosty Monday morning, he flung his arms around me, completely out of the blue, and told me he had some big, big news for me. That tickled me in itself, as it was an expression we used a lot as a family. Was it proof that he was finally melting into the fabric of ours? I hoped so.

'So what is it, then, this big, big news of yours, Spencer?' I asked laughing, as he finished giving me his knock-you-down hug.

'That I really like living with you an' Mike now,' he told me. 'I hated it at first, but not any more.' And with that he skipped happily into school.

Just as well, really, because all I could get out was 'and we love having you' before my throat became jammed with an unexpected lump. Not a cool state to be in at the school gates.

It was the first thing I wanted to tell John an hour later, when he called to see how the home visit had gone.

But I was stopped in my tracks even before I could get so much as a word out. John wasn't, it turned out, calling to find out about the weekend. Quite the opposite. It was in fact to fill *me* in.

'I've got bad news, I'm afraid,' was almost the first thing he said to me, knocking my happy mood straight into touch.

'Bad?' I asked, noticing the heavy sigh that had gone with it. 'What's happened? How bad is bad, John?'

'Pretty bad,' he said. 'Bottom line, Casey, is that I've had Glenn on the phone for half an hour this morning. Seems the Herringtons were on to social services first thing. They've decided they don't want Spencer back.'

'What?' I gasped, stunned. 'What, *ever*?'

'I know,' John said. 'I can hardly believe it myself. But they're adamant, Glenn says, especially after this weekend.'

This brought me up short. 'But how can that be? What are you talking about? The visit went so well. Well, compared to the last two, for sure. Spencer was so happy when we picked him up.'

'Er, that's not quite the way the Herringtons have described it, Casey. According to them it was a nightmare, and they're now saying seeing him is having a detrimental effect on the other kids.'

*Oh, and her drinking isn't?* I thought, though I bit my tongue and didn't say it. But I was aghast at this development. How could there be so much disparity between what they said and Spencer said? 'How?' I asked John. 'How was it a nightmare?'

'As in he bit his little sister on the face,' John explained. 'As in he threw hot spaghetti at one of his brothers. They're adamant, Casey. No point in us railing against it. Got to think of what's going to be best for young Spencer. No point trying to get him home if they've completely washed their hands of him.'

'I know,' I said, feeling the upset and anger throb like a pulse in my temple. How could they do that? How could they just abandon their own flesh and blood? All too easily, came the reply of the realist inside me. Happened all the time. Hadn't I seen it first hand? 'But what now? And how am I going to tell him? You know he's going to react …'

'Pretty badly, I know. Poor kid. But don't worry. I'm not going to leave you to deal with that on your own. Wouldn't be fair. No, we're going to have to start looking for a long-term placement for him. But don't you break it to him. That needs to come from me. How about I come over for when you get back from the school run this afternoon? Would that be okay for you? Softly, softly, of course. I won't lay it on the line in one hit. Oh, and I almost forgot. Did he say anything to you about a guinea pig? Apparently they're short of one of theirs and Kerry Herrington's saying Spencer might have let it out of the cage on purpose.'

'No,' I said. 'I didn't even know they had any bloody guinea pigs!' I felt a fleeting and mirthless smile cross my features. What irony. 'They're clearly as good at keeping an eye on guinea pigs as they are children, eh, John? But no.' I finished, thinking, *Well, tough, frankly Kerry* ... 'He didn't come back with one stuffed up his jumper, if that's what they expected ... I think I would have noticed if he had done, don't you?'

*Maybe it took itself off to social services*, I thought wryly. Unprofessional, I knew, because Kerry Herrington clearly needed help. But Spencer needed *more* help. So I couldn't help it.

Upset though I was as the hours ticked by till home time, I grew more resigned. Yes, I'd be left to pick up the pieces in the short term, which I could hardly bear to think about, but, ultimately, if his parents – particularly his mother – didn't want him then Spencer would be better off without them. If they'd truly set their minds on it there was nothing I could do, and, in any case, I'd seen the sort of damage that could be done to a child when they were allowed to keep hoping when all hope was lost. Or, worse, kept being given hope by parents who seesawed between wanting their kid back and then changing their minds again. If this was the final cut, better it happen and be done with it, so that poor Spencer could have a shot at building a new, more settled life. Still, my mood was at least productive. I polished the whole house into sparkling submission, though no amount of furious dusting could help me answer the simple question – why?

I hated picking him up. I felt so devious and dishonest, responding to his chirpy chatter about his day with an equally jolly manner of my own, pretending everything was normal, when 'normal' was about as far removed from this child's life as it was possible to be.

'What's he want?' Spencer asked as we pulled up outside the house to see John, who'd now spotted us, get out of his car. He sighed theatrically. 'What have I done *now*?'

'I don't know love,' I lied, keeping my voice light, though my stomach was churning. As well it might. There was no doubt that in a very short time the rest of the day was going to morph into an emotional nightmare. 'Nothing, I'm sure,' I said. 'Anyway, we'll see, won't we? Why don't you go straight up and get out of your uniform while I get you a drink and see why he's here?'

Spencer trotted off happily enough. He was clearly not that bothered by John's arrival, which made the disparity between the two reports of the home visit feel even stranger. If he'd done what they'd said, surely alarm bells would be ringing? Or was this all another facet of the sociopath tag? I didn't know it, but I was about to have my mind somewhat concentrated in that regard, and how.

I gathered milk and biscuits, then pulled down mugs and brewed coffee, while John stood, hands in pockets, looking every inch the man with a necessary but deeply unpleasant job to do. And it was a look I could see was beginning to impact on Spencer as he returned to the kitchen and looked at us both.

'Let's go and all of us sit at the table, shall we?' I told him. 'Have a snack while John has a little chat with us.'

Spencer sat, as directed, now looking plainly anxious. I was grateful that John didn't beat around the bush. 'Spencer,' he began, 'there are some things I have to say to you, but two things first – one is that you need to listen to what I'm going to say very carefully, and the other is that you understand that none of this is your fault, okay?' Spencer nodded silently, his big brown eyes looking huge in his pale face. I watched his hand gripping his glass a little harder.

'So Spencer, the thing is,' John began, 'that for the time being the contact sessions with your family have to stop ...' He paused, as if waiting for a response, but there was none. Spencer just continued to watch him, immobile. 'They haven't been going too well, you see, have they? And, well, your mum hasn't been coping as well as we'd hoped. The thing is, Spencer, that, well, until the grown-ups work everything out, you might have to stay in care ... *will* have to stay in care for longer than we'd hoped, which will mean' – he glanced at me now – 'us finding you a different, long-term family. A family who are used to taking care of kids for longer periods than Casey and Mike do, and who ...'

It was like a bomb had been detonated, so completely was the sound of John's voice drowned out. 'Nooooo!' Spencer roared. 'Nooo!' he raged, leaping to his feet and sending his glass of milk flying. 'Fuck that! Fuck you! I'm going home and you can't stop me!' He launched himself at John then, punching him and kicking him while screaming obscenities. 'Fuck you! I hate you! I fucking hate you all!'

John did his best to defend himself and to try and restrain Spencer, while I jumped up and tried to calm him down too. Within moments John had Spencer pinned against him, his body facing outwards, his legs still thrashing out like pistons and his feet catching me sporadically, as he kicked out. 'Come on, love,' I pleaded with him. 'This won't help, will it? Spencer, you're going to hurt yourself. Please, love. Please stop. It's not John's fault.'

'I hate you!' he screamed at me. 'I hate you. I hate you! You're s'posed to fix me but you're rubbish. You can't fix no kids. You're stupid and I hate you! I HATE you!'

The tears sprang in my eyes as I watched his face contort, deformed by the pain that was coursing through his body. How much hurt could one small child endure, for God's sake? How devastating must it be to be told your parents don't want you? Just you. Not your siblings. Just you. You alone. Discarded. And so easily. Just by means of a phone call, leaving the Johns of the world – not to mention the likes of me and Mike – to deal with the devastating fall-out.

'Love,' I kept repeating, '*please* stop. This isn't John's fault. Please love, calm down so we can talk all this through. Try to explain things to you …'

'Like what?' he yelled, tears streaming down scarlet cheeks now. He was still jerking himself backwards, trying to hurt John. 'Like nobody wants me? Well, fine. I don't need no one. I can take care of myself. Let me go an' I can go an' get my stuff and get out of here, and you can tell my mum I'm glad what I did to the fucking guinea pig!'

The guinea pig. I looked at John. Oh, God, so it *was* true. Spencer's expression confirmed it. His eyes were wild.

'Spencer ...' I started.

'Yeah, I took it,' he screeched. 'An' it's dead an' I'm glad!'

As he said this John must have loosened his grip temporarily, because Spencer suddenly broke free and thundered off up the stairs. John, catching his breath, as I was, shook his head.

'Casey, leave him. He can't get out from up there, can he?'

'Actually, he can,' I corrected him. 'Through the skylight, remember?'

I headed out of the room and started up the stairs. I soon realised that Spencer hadn't gone into his bedroom. He'd gone into the bathroom. Perhaps he was being sick. It wouldn't have surprised me at all. He was in such a state.

But it at least meant he wasn't about to scarper again. 'Oh, God, John,' I said, turning, as he followed me up the stairs. 'Oh *God* – something's just occurred to me. The box –'

'What box?'

'The box he brought back on Saturday,' I panted. 'The box he said was full of his dinosaur books. It's in the shed ...'

John frowned. 'Okay, you go up and deal with Spencer,' he said. 'I'm not going to help anything. I'm the messenger, remember? You go and talk to him and I'll go out to the shed and have a look.' He ploughed his hair back into place. He looked like he'd just lost a prize fight. Up on the landing, the bathroom door, predictably, was locked. I could hear Spencer sobbing but he wouldn't respond to me. I racked my brains for ways he could harm himself in there, but could find none except the obvious, because we'd been fostering too long now to be anything less than hyper-vigilant in such matters. And I could hear no water running, in any case. My hunch was that Spencer wouldn't do that to himself anyway. Perhaps he just needed to cry it out for a bit. Which was fine. I could sit here for as long as that took.

I was still listening at the door when John reappeared down in the hall with the box. His expression was questioning as he started up the stairs again. 'This it?'

I nodded dumbly as he approached. 'I can hardly bear to –'

'Phew. You won't have to,' he said, opening it and as he did so flapping his hand to stir the air in front of his face. Sure enough, one guinea pig. Entombed. And very dead.

The following few days were just terrible. It had taken over an hour to coax Spencer out of the bathroom, and he was in such a state I couldn't even begin to think about bringing up the guinea pig. By the time I'd got him out, I had already sent John away, and asked him to deal with the poor animal before he left.

But it weighed heavily. First there'd been the little girl whose head Spencer had calmly held under the water, and now this. This horrible interment of a family pet. It was a chilling image, a chilling concept. Perhaps the psychologist was right. Perhaps Spencer *was* a sociopath. Perhaps he had been born evil after all.

I hated my thoughts, but what sort of person could do that? The answer, of course, was staring me in the face. A very hurt, profoundly damaged child, that's who. Of which I'd already had experience in our first foster child, Justin. Some kids lash out, some kids self-harm, some do both. Justin, aged five, had burned down his family home, deliberately killing his mother's much-loved dog in the process, to pay her back for destroying his own, then short, life, not only through cruelty and staggering neglect but also by making him perform sexual favours for her pushers, to get her hands on her drugs.

No, I thought, you didn't need to be a sociopath to do the things Spencer had done. Just be very, very damaged and distressed.

But was it a life sentence? Not necessarily. Justin was fine now. Though he was never going to fully integrate in the wider world of close relationships, much less within his family, he was a functioning, working adult with a decent quality of life now – and still very much a part of *our* family. Whatever ailed Spencer, we shouldn't give up hope.

Nevertheless, bearing witness first hand to what he'd done made it hard to function normally around him. We also decided not to tell Kieron, which made it even harder. We knew he'd be appalled. I hated being the keeper of such a horrible secret.

Spencer himself kept his counsel. He was able to calm down sufficiently by the following afternoon that John was

able to pop back round, sit down with him and talk to him
both about what he'd done to the guinea pig – which he
approached with great delicacy – and what would happen,
in the short term, to Spencer himself.

But I could see Spencer withdrawing into himself,
slowly but oh so surely. Saw his glazed expression, conceal-
ing I'm sure a maelstrom of feelings, which he'd clearly
decided there was no longer any point in sharing. He went
to school each day, worked hard – they said so daily – and
came home again, and interacted with us superficially
normally. But it was as if the door that I'd been ever so
slowly inching open had now been locked again, and I no
longer had a key. And perhaps I never would now. It
certainly seemed so.

John, in the meantime, had been busy. Given the incident with the guinea pig and the need to prepare a report
ready for a new placement, he'd arranged with Glenn that
Spencer be seen again by the psychologist, in an attempt to
learn anything extra that could be fathomed about what
was going on in his head.

'And what about Penny?' I asked him, when he called to
run through the latest update. The one thing Spencer had
asked me was when he might next be going swimming.

'Well, for the time being they've decided to put that on
hold. Her workload's huge as it is, and until we're
completely sure what we're dealing with … well, you know
how things are with the budget. Though, fingers crossed,
once we get the latest report back from the psychologist …
Which brings me to the next thing.'

'Which is?'

Which was – and we'd known this was coming: how could it not be? – that John wanted to know if Mike and I would hang on to Spencer for a little while longer.

'What with everything,' he said, apologetically, 'it's going to be tricky, as you can imagine now, moving forward.'

'That's fine,' I said. 'Of course. Finding suitably robust and experienced carers will be a challenge, we appreciate that. Especially ones young enough and energetic enough to cope with him. He's not the sort of child who's going to work well with an older couple, I don't think.'

'Well, actually, it's not that,' he said. 'It's really that things have changed now.' With which words he then delivered his final blow. 'We're not looking for mainstream foster carers,' he said. 'Not any more. You've probably guessed, haven't you?'

'No,' I said. Because I hadn't. 'You're not looking for long-term specialists?'

'No,' he said. 'It was an option, but, well, we're all agreed now. No. It's been a hard decision to reach, but the consensus is that we have little choice, given everything that's happened. We're looking to find him – well, for the foreseeable future anyway – a place in a secure unit somewhere.'

I was aghast. He was eight! It simply hadn't occurred to me that someone so young could be considered for somewhere like that. They were places for violent, disturbed teenagers, weren't they? Dangerous adolescents. I said as much to John.

'We've no choice,' he told me again. 'This is a child who already displays very dangerous behaviours. To do anything else would be irresponsible. Fire-fighting, really. It wouldn't be fair to place him just anywhere, you know that.'

And the tragedy was that I did. He was right. As much as others would need protection from Spencer, he really did need protection from himself. And as John explained, these places were set up to deal with these extreme kids. They had resources to which the fostering service might never have access.

'Best place,' John finished. 'For now, at least. You know that.'

And I did, but I couldn't help but think about that guinea pig. Once Spencer was incarcerated in such a place, in that system, what chance was there he'd ever live a normal life again? Minuscule, we both knew. I was heartbroken.

# Chapter 19

If I was heartbroken, Spencer was just, well, broken. Hurtling in that direction, anyway. It really seemed that now he knew he wasn't going home again, he was determined to show us just how 'evil' he could be, doing that thing that, distressingly, children could do so well: obliging everyone who thought only the very worst of him, by turning into the monster he'd now officially been labelled. He really did seem to be on a path to self-destruction. As the next few days passed – in something of a haze for me – it seemed there was a constant stream of misdemeanours being reported by the neighbours. He broke two cars' wing mirrors; he kicked a cat; he beat another child up. Like Pavlov's dogs, I too was becoming conditioned – to be traumatised every time I heard the doorbell.

As his carers, Mike and my role in the current situation was clear. While John and Glenn began exploring the options in terms of finding a secure unit that would take such a young boy, we had to stick rigidly, as we'd been doing, to the behaviour modification programme, however hollow or pointless it now seemed.

And it did feel pretty pointless. Sticking to the rules put us in the ridiculous situation where whatever misdemeanour Spencer had been responsible for could only be punished by him failing to earn peer time, and, knowing how things worked, he could use his single night of grounding to earn sufficient points that he could play out again the next night, and so the crazy cycle would continue.

Not for the first time, I questioned the efficacy of the system. Yes, for a child struggling with impulsive and destructive behaviours the actions/consequences and rewards model worked really well, giving that child a sense that they could take control of their *own* lives – in most cases, with kids who'd been 'controlled' by the system, or a difficult home life, this was key to building autonomy and self-esteem, and so to making progress.

But when a child understood the points system, and was determined to play it to suit their own ends, it became point*less*. All Spencer was learning was that if he earned sufficient points he had autonomy to do what he liked.

'It's mad,' Mike observed, as he shut the living-room curtains one Saturday afternoon, having just called Spencer in to have a bath before tea. It was the back end of November now – we were rushing headlong towards December – but I didn't feel Christmassy at all. Not with Spencer's future still undecided and hanging over us. Pointless was exactly how the whole situation felt. Now that we'd had it spelled out that there was to be no positive outcome for him, it was as if we'd become more like prison guards than carers hoping to help him. And I was sure he felt this too. When Spencer was in, he behaved impeccably so that he could earn the points he needed, but because of his behaviour once he was out – mostly naughty – it was as if Mike and I had been put in charge of the exercise hour in a maximum-security prison – we were constantly on edge, waiting for the next bout of trouble.

'I know, love,' I said, 'but what else can we do? It's –'

'Uh-oh,' Mike interrupted me. 'What's all this, then?'

I joined him at the window to see a police car had pulled up, and had also disgorged two officers, who seemed to be inspecting the local cars. Seemed like we were about to find some more.

Mike was at the front door before the policemen – two uniformed officers – had finished walking up our front path. It had become almost instinctive. Get them inside quickly before too many people realised that the patrol car up the road was anything to do with us.

I braced myself for the worst as we invited them in. 'Is this about Spencer?' Mike asked as we ushered them into the living room, closing the door behind us so that Spencer, up in the bath, wasn't alerted.

The taller of them nodded as he sat down. 'Does the lad own a slingshot?' he wanted to know. Mike and I glanced at each other, puzzled. 'Not that we know of,' I answered. 'What's happened?'

He frowned. 'I suspect he might have,' he said. 'Because we've had a number of complaints from several of your neighbours, and they all report it having been fired from a top window in your house.'

And causing quite a lot of damage, by all accounts. 'Damage to parked cars, in the main,' the other officer told us, which explained their earlier inspections. 'That your car out the front?' He asked. 'The dark-green one?' Mike nodded. 'Because one of your neighbours seemed to be under the impression that he's been firing stones at your car as well.'

Mike leapt up. 'What? The little … God!'

It only took a couple of minutes to confirm it. If what the policemen said was true, Spencer did indeed have a slingshot, and had been entertaining himself with it for some time. Was there no end to the ways he could find to live up to his label? It was as if he'd decided there was just no point in doing otherwise any more.

'What I'd suggest,' the other officer said, after I'd explained a little of our situation as Spencer's foster carers, 'is that you bring him down and that we speak to him. And, with your permission, get just a little bit heavy. Eight years old, you say? Well, then, I'd suggest that if we put the fear of God into him we might nip the actions of our little Dennis the Menace in the bud.'

We both agreed. This wasn't unusual. We'd plenty of experience with these sorts of tactics. Sometimes boys with a tendency to go off the rails could be reined in successfully using nothing more drastic than just a scary dressing down from someone in a uniform.

And these two clearly had as well. After bringing Spencer down – and, in Mike's case, the anger which accompanied this wasn't embellished for effect, either: he was furious – I had to keep reminding myself, as they laid into him about his behaviour, that, as far as they were concerned, anyway, this was all for his own good. And though privately, initially, I had my doubts about that (this was no ordinary eight-year-old) as they railed at him about law breaking and how likely it was he'd end up in prison, I found myself getting quite upset, as they clearly *were* getting through to him; after ten minutes, his face wet with tears, he actually buried his head in my lap, and, try as I might, I could not prise it back up again.

Sensing he was having the desired effect, the angry policeman took a step closer to Spencer's ear. 'And if you think *this* is bad,' he hissed, 'just wait till you see what happens *next* time, my lad.'

I was shocked, then, when Spencer slowly *did* lift his face, and even more so when I realised he hadn't been crying at all – he'd actually been laughing. He even smiled at the policeman as he drew his own conclusion. 'I'm too young to fucking prosecute, you muppet!'

To his credit, the astonished officer hardly paused to draw breath. And this time his fury was genuine. Wrenching Spencer up by his pyjama collar he virtually roared into his face. 'You look at me when I'm speaking to you, boy! You hear me? Don't you *dare* try to speak to me like that! Now, I don't know where you've got your information from, but just you try me. Let's just see who's right and who's wrong about that, shall we? Because' – and here he shook Spencer, just a little, but enough to wipe the smile from his face – 'if I have to come back here – and you can definitely take this as a warning – for any reason *whatsoever*, trust me, I *will* arrest you. And I'll sling you in a cell!'

Finally, I thought. Finally, he's scared and he's listening. Finally, the policeman seemed to be making an impression. 'Now get out of my sight,' he snapped. 'Go on, get to your room and stay there! How dare you treat these good people with such complete disrespect? Go on, hoppit, before I change my mind and arrest you now after all.'

Spencer didn't need any prompting to make good an escape; he was up the stairs like a whippet, and for a moment the four of us just stared after him. And then stared at each other, and I think we were all thinking the same thing. If he was like this at eight, and given the tragic start he was having, what did he have the potential to become once he'd got a couple more years under his belt?

There was no point in giving the two officers chapter and verse about the grim future that was already being mapped out for him. Instead, we let them go thinking they'd gone some way, anyway, towards truncating at least one life of juvenile petty crime.

But we knew differently, and it turned into a sombre Saturday evening, Mike, in a foul mood about the dents in his car, and me preoccupied with typing up yet more incident reports which I would then forward to John and John would forward to social services and which would just add to the growing pile of evidence, already weighty, that this was a child for whom nothing very much could be done. Just born evil. End of. And in the system.

I was normally a great one for saying 'tomorrow's another day' but when I woke on Sunday morning my usual 'sleeves up and crack on' mentality had seemed to desert me.

Instead the pointlessness of our current situation with Spencer seemed to hang over the household like a pall of left-over firework night smoke.

Not that there had been any more fireworks. I had gone up to take Spencer some sandwiches and a drink, half-expecting him to have packed a hankie on the end of a stick and disappeared, like some sort of pantomime runaway. However, he was very much present, and very purposely turned over in his bed to face the wall, clearly in no mood for a chat. In the end I simply left the tray on his bedside table without saying anything, because I was really in no mood to chat to him either. Better, I decided, to leave him to his own thoughts and digest what the policeman had told him. But I didn't get any satisfaction from seeing him so chastised. All states were temporary with Spencer, as we'd seen before. He'd keep his head down, act contrite, and then return to his default – his new default, now he knew he wasn't going to be going home, of doing what he liked and to hell with the consequences. And what could I do for him? What could I do to try and change things? What miracle might happen that would change the trajectory of his life?

Make breakfast, in the short term, I told myself grimly. Make breakfast and then see what could be salvaged from the wreckage of the weekend. So, leaving Mike showering, I went down to cook bacon and sausages.

That done, and with still no sign of either Mike or, indeed, Spencer, I called up the stairs. 'Mike, love, can you knock Spencer up, please? I'm ready to put some eggs on.'

But my hand was still poised over the frying pan, egg in hand, when Mike called back down to me.

'Love, you there? I think you'd better get up here.'

*Oh God*, I thought, for all my *que sera* attitude the previous evening. *He's not done a runner again, has he?*

'Where's Spencer?' I called as I headed into the hallway. Why wouldn't he? He hardly had much to stay for now, did he? Even less if he knew what was presently being planned for him: a place that he *couldn't* escape from. No, with social services not allowing us to screw down his window – which I had no choice but to accept, even though I wasn't convinced it constituted a fire escape: we had plenty of other windows upstairs, after all – there was always an exit route for Spencer, if he really wanted one. He wasn't in that secure unit yet, after all. Cross though I was, though, I still couldn't help thinking, *Okay then, to hell with it. If that's what you want, so be it.*

But I was wrong. 'Oh, he's right here,' Mike answered. '*Right* here. I mean get up here and see what he's *done*.'

# Chapter 20

It probably said a lot about the sort of things I'd witnessed since we began fostering, but when I reached Spencer's bedroom to find he'd completely trashed it my principal feeling was one of relief. I don't know quite what I had expected to find – the body of another guinea pig? Something larger? A local dog? The sight of a small, hapless, terrified child, whom he'd kidnapped, tied up and was busy torturing?

Possibly not, but even so, I was relieved. I remembered back to previous kids we'd looked after and some of the things they had done; it was undeniably upsetting, knowing a distressed child had destroyed their belongings and their environment – not to mention annoying; this was wanton destruction, after all – but in the big scheme of things I had seen far, far worse; children whose pain was too great to be made better by hurting *things* – they had felt compelled instead to set upon their own bodies. This was not that, and I found myself grateful. So it was necessary to do a quick mental recalibration in order to change my expression to one that was more appropriate.

'Spencer,' I asked rhetorically, since it was obvious, 'what have you done?'

He was sitting on the edge of his bed, absently stroking his Fluffy Cow puppet, who was on one hand, and glaring defiantly at Mike. Now he turned his head to face me, but his expression was blank. Well, almost. *Isn't that obvious?*, it seemed to say.

I duly took in the scene. He had made rips in numerous items of clothing, including what looked like most of his school uniform and his cherished Aston Villa football shirt. Toys and games were strewn all over the floor, many of them obviously broken beyond repair, including his precious DS, which I could see was now minus its screen. The carpet was sprinkled with a pot-pourri of bits and pieces – jigsaw pieces, mostly, plus Lego bricks and various counters, along with countless pens and pencils which he'd clearly systematically snapped in half. He'd even snapped what looked like all his paintbrushes in half, which upset me the most. He was so gifted. Why would he *do* that? Because painting pictures felt pointless when you didn't have adoring parents to tell you just what a clever boy you were?

But my eye understandably was drawn to the wall on which the picture – the one he'd created his hidey-hole behind – usually hung. It no longer did. It was propped against the opposite wall, while the space behind it, which Mike had so painstakingly re-plastered, was once again the site of a huge gaping hole, beneath which was a small mound of gouged-out paint and plaster.

What struck me most, however, was that he had done this overnight, and neither of us had heard a single thing. So this wasn't the result of a child in a rage, busy venting his anger or distress. He'd done all this carefully, methodically, quietly. I wished I had the first idea what had been going through his mind. Was this to hurt us? The policemen? An act of defiance or one of regret?

'Spencer?' I said again. Once again he said nothing. Instead he leapt from the bed, pushed past us and thundered down the stairs.

I followed him out onto the landing. 'Don't you dare go out of that front door, d'you hear me?' I shouted after him. 'I mean it. You stay right there and wait for us to come down.' He was hovering in the hallway, and, presumably because he was still in his nightclothes, seemed undecided about doing a flit in any case. Even so, I decided to press my point anyway. His winter coat was hanging only inches away from him, after all. 'Because if you do,' I said, giving my expression both barrels, 'I will ground you for a month. No ifs and buts, no discussion, no totting up of points. Sod the bloody points,' I added. 'Got that?'

Evidently yes. He darted into the living room.

'God,' said Mike, who was still sitting on the bed, looking world-weary. 'What are we going to *do* with this bloody kid, Case? How long's he been with us now? Four months? Nearly five now, isn't it?' He stood up, and went to inspect the gaping wound in the wall. 'Talk about one step forward, two steps back … No. I take that back. Talk about *no* steps forward, period.' He shook his head as he peered into the hole.

'I know, love,' I said, already wondering what I was going to send him into school in, in the morning. 'We'll talk to him. On the plus side, this is at least straightforward. He gets a rollicking from the police, he trashes his bedroom. Cause and effect.' I stooped to pick up a favourite hoodie, which he'd managed to wrench the sleeves from. 'Well, that's his day mapped out, anyway. Bit of a job on, clearing this lot. Hey, close that window, love, will you?' I said, as the blind inside the skylight starting banging against the dormer in the bitter wind. 'It's bloody freezing in here. Like an ice box.'

Mike stepped past me. 'I'm going to see if I can fix this,' he said, standing on the bed to reach up to it. 'See if I can find some way of securing it without breaking any rules, like a safety latch, so that it only opens partly. Because when he opens it, he always …' There was a long pause. 'What the *hell*?'

I turned. Mike had his head sticking out of the window and could obviously see something I couldn't. 'What, love?' I asked him. 'What is it?'

He popped is head back inside. 'I think I've just found Spencer's latest hiding place. There's plastic bags all along the guttering out here. All neatly tied up and …' he was glancing around. 'Pass me something up, can you? Just something I can reach down and hook them up with. I can almost reach, but … there.' he pointed. 'Grab me that, will you?'

I followed his gaze, and saw a fishing net on a bamboo cane. I grabbed it. 'Let me see,' I said, climbing up on to the bed too, as I passed him it.

'Hang on,' he said, feeding the cane out. 'I'll pass them in to you. Bloody hell, Case. Who'd have thought it? It's like the checkout at Tesco out here.'

As Mike passed the wet, tatty bags back in through the window, I began to open them. I went gingerly, at first, fearful that they might also harbour spiders. But I soon realised that no spider – not one with any sense, anyway – would make its home in the folds of a freezing carrier bag, in a freezing gutter, on a freezing roof.

They'd been well tied, too. The contents of all were clean and dry. And somewhat astonishing, and not in a good way. Pouches of tobacco – many full, cigarette lighters, packs of matches, items of jewellery, video games, CDs and DVDs … even a pristine pair of adult-sized trainers. I stared in confusion as, finally, Mike jumped back down. 'What on earth does this all mean?' I wanted to know.

'I think we both know the answer to that,' he said. 'He's been thieving again, hasn't he? Up to his old tricks, that's what. Jesus –' He shook his head. 'It's a wonder he hasn't slipped and killed himself, in this weather.'

A shiver ran through me, as an image of Spencer's lifeless broken body on our front lawn leapt into my mind. 'Oh, love, don't say that,' I said. 'God, I can't believe this, I really can't.'

Mike shut the skylight and, in spite of everything, even managed a chuckle. '*What? Love, I honestly can't believe you *said* that,' he replied.

Back downstairs, we found Spencer curled up in a small ball in a corner of the sofa, his arms wrapped round his knees and an expression of sullen defiance still on his face. It changed very quickly, however, once he eyed the dozen or so bags Mike was holding. His eyes widened, visibly, and his mouth opened. Not to speak, just to form a silent 'uh-oh'. And at that moment I could practically see the mechanisms of his mind working. He started to blink and I just knew that he was wondering how he was supposed to get out of this one.

Mike crossed the room and dumped the bags on the floor in front of him. 'No point in lying to us, lad,' he said. 'I need to know where this lot's come from. *Now*. Come on lad, spill. You've lived with us long enough now to know this won't be dropped till I get to the bottom of it, so you might as well save us all some time and energy by getting on with it. Well?'

But it was as if Spencer was on autopilot. 'Dunno,' he said. 'It's not mine.' He then turned away and sank his head further into his lap, like a toddler trying to make himself 'invisible'.

'I said no lies,' Mike responded, both evenly and calmly. Despite that, I knew he wasn't far off losing his temper. I decided to try and help.

'Look, love, we know this stuff was put up there by you, so you might as well own up. Spencer, think about it. It'll be so much better for you to be honest, because if you own up you're not going to lose even more points for telling lies and being disrespectful, are you? So the consequences won't be as severe.' I didn't dare glance at Mike because I knew exactly what his expression would be; I didn't need to see, I could feel his eyes rolling. He always hated that the kids might misinterpret my reasoning as me being a bit of a soft touch.

But Spencer at least answered. 'Why d'you always think it's me, eh? That kid next door had been nicking all sorts. It's prob'ly him. The police have been after him and everything.' He unclasped his arms now, warming to his story. 'It's prob'ly him,' he said again. 'I did see all that stuff on the roof. But I never said owt, because I'm not a *grass*.'

He was really getting into his stride now. Having hit upon what he obviously felt was a plausible explanation, he looked almost animated now. His tone implied that this was a matter of some pride, which we should appreciate. His hands were tied. It was as if he was some old prison-hardened lag.

The kid next door, though? *Really?* The kid next door – there was only one; on the other side of us there was an older couple – couldn't have been more than seven or so. And a normal seven-year-old. Nothing at all like Spencer.

Mike wasn't fazed in the least, however. 'Next door, you say?' he asked Spencer, beginning to gather the bags into his hands again. 'Okay, lad, come with me then. We'll go and settle this right now.'

Spencer looked stricken. 'But I'm in my jamas!'

'No matter,' said Mike, almost cheerfully. 'It's only next door. Come on. Up you get, son.'

After a sorrowful glance in my direction, which I pretended not to notice, Spencer followed Mike out into the hall. He had his head hung to his chest and looked a pitiful sight as he trudged behind Mike to the front door. It being Sunday, I too was still in my pyjamas – Mike was the only one dressed. I grabbed my housecoat from the back of a dining chair and pushed my arms into the sleeves as I followed to watch what happened from our own doorstep; we were in semis that were configured so the front doors were only a few feet apart.

Our next-door neighbours on the left had only lived there for a couple of weeks. And though I'd said the usual hellos when the family had moved in, I'd since seen almost nothing of any of them. The door was opened by the father, a large man who looked to be in his early thirties, and who looked understandably puzzled to see his new next-door neighbour on his doorstep bearing supermarket carrier bags. He looked no less confused when Mike explained why he and Spencer were there. It was only when Mike began showing him the bags' contents that the penny dropped. Now confusion was replaced by growing anger.

'What's going on, mate?' he asked Mike as yet another bag seemed to contain items he recognised. 'They're my trainers!' he gasped. 'And that's my bloody baccy!'

'Well,' said Mike, 'we don't actually know where these things have come from, only that they were in the gutter outside Spencer here's bedroom.'

The man now looked hard at Spencer, who seemed to visibly shrink. 'You done this, then?' he snapped. 'You been in my bloody house again? How many times do you need telling?'

'Again?' asked Mike, before Spencer could reply.

'Yeah, again,' the man said. 'Seems so. Despite me telling you' – he thrust a finger in Spencer's direction – 'to clear off and keep away from my son.'

'Again?' asked Mike again. Like me, he was clearly confused. As far as we knew, Spencer had yet to make the little boy's acquaintance. We'd certainly not seen him or heard him mentioned.

'Oh, I suppose you didn't know. Caught the little blighter and my lad nicking tools out my shed. Another place I told you to keep your thieving mitts out of!'

'I didn't take that stuff!' Spencer interrupted. Both men looked hard at him. 'I didn't! How could I have when I'm not even allowed in your house?'

Back on my own doorstep I had a heart-sinking thought. That he might not need the sort of access most kids did – i.e. through a door. That he'd been galloping over the roofs again. It seemed obvious.

'Well, it's got into your grubby little hands somehow, hasn't it?' the man demanded.

'I tell you I never touched that stuff!' Spencer persisted. He was crying now. 'Go get your Chrissy. Ask him. He'll tell you it wasn't me.'

Chrissy, the man's son, was duly summoned to the doorstep. He was a waif of a child, compared to Spencer. Barely looked seven. Might have been as young as six, even. He looked terrified, as well he might. I watched as Spencer, clearly pleased to see him, placed a hand on his shoulder. 'Don't be scared, mate,' he said gently. 'This is important, though. Just tell your dad how you took this stuff and threw it all down the roof. They all think *I* did it, and I'm already in trouble with the cops. So if you don't tell the truth I'm gonna get arrested. Go on. It'll be all right. Just tell the truth, okay?'

I looked on with a mounting unease. He looked every inch the experienced social worker or a skilfully persuasive police officer, perhaps, trying to coax a confession out of an errant child. We all stood and waited for the response, which came quickly. I don't know what I expected. I don't know what any of us expected. For the boy to burst out crying? Shriek a denial? Refuse to speak?

He did none of those. He calmly turned to his father and did as instructed. 'It was me, Dad. I did it,' he said.

'Chrissy,' his father said, grabbing the bags up from where Mike had placed them on the doorstep. 'There is NO WAY you did this. What are you scared of?' he pointed at Spencer, who was retreating back now, towards our doorway. 'You scared of this little runt? Is that it? Well, don't be. You don't have to listen to anything *he* has to say, lad, I can assure you.'

The boy shook his head. 'I did it, Dad, honest. Just for a joke. I was going to give it all back, honest I was.'

'Get in the fucking house!' his dad shouted, clearly exasperated by this turn of events. 'And as for you,' he snarled at Spencer. 'You stay away from us, you hear? I catch you round here again, catch you *anywhere* near my kid again, I'll be sorting you out myself – got that?' He then turned to Mike. 'You got that, too, mate?'

But there was no time for Mike to answer. Before he could open his mouth to speak, the man had gone back inside and slammed the door.

'Great,' said Mike, as he followed us both back in. 'Always nice to make friends with new neighbours, eh, Spencer?'

Spencer turned to him, looking utterly guileless and innocent. 'See?' he said. 'I told you it wasn't me.' He then actually put his hands on his hips, shook his head and rolled his eyes. And, nodding in the direction of next door, he sighed. 'Phew. What a carry-on, though, eh?'

Neither of us really knew where to start. Much as both of us knew he was lying through his teeth, without any evidence, and with a clear admission of guilt from the other child, there was really very little we could do. Yes, we could lecture him about acting as a handler of stolen goods for his 'mate' Chrissy, and we could make it clear that we thought he was a liar. But to what end? He could continue to deny it till literally the very day John came and took him – to whatever grim institution he was able to line up for him. Which made it all feel as hollow as the points system did now – completely pointless. A waste of time. How was it going to help anything?

No, what I needed to do, if there was anything I *could* do, was find my way past the wrongdoings to the heart of the problem. And that *was* the problem. We'd been here since day one. And since his circumstances had changed so much – and so much for the worse – what of use could we hope to achieve? That when he got to wherever he was going, in the midst of his abandonment, he'd learned not to tell fibs and nick from neighbours? I thought not.

We did eat our breakfast, because, for one, we were all hungry, and as we did so Mike spelled out to Spencer that for as long as it took he would stay in his bedroom where, supervised by me, he'd restore it to exactly how it had been before he'd trashed it. He would also, we made clear, be expected to pay for the things he'd broken, by doing extra chores, to earn extra pocket money, which we'd deduct on a weekly basis. The same also applied to his school uniform.

Spencer didn't argue about any of this. He seemed satisfied he'd achieved the result he needed – that poor Chrissy had owned up and let him off the hook. And who knew? Did he have a lucrative sideline on the go? What was the plan for all the rooftop contraband, anyway? We'd probably never know; until Spencer decided to own up to nicking it, all we could expect to hear would be fabrications. We took up black bags and green bags and the vacuum and various sprays and cloths, and he set to work happily enough, as instructed, while I sorted washing and stripped our bed and generally pottered on the landing, keeping half an eye on what was happening in his bedroom.

God, I thought, the police visit felt like ages ago now. Would that be the way now – that we just tripped from misdemeanour to misdemeanour, docking pocket money as required, till the day came when this tragic child left us? I looked in on him. He had his back to me, kneeling on the floor, collecting up the pieces of a jigsaw, a space scene from *Star Wars*, a puzzle I'd got, like so many toys we'd bought for our foster kids, from my favourite local charity shop. I wasn't sure if he'd actually completed it. Wasn't sure if he'd started it, even. Perhaps he never would now.

'D'you think you'll find all the bits?' I asked him.

He swivelled. He hadn't heard me. His eyes I noticed, with shock, belied his earlier demeanour. They were red raw. He'd obviously been crying silently, but hard. Real tears. Not crocodile, switch-on, switch-off ones. Did sociopaths cry like this? When they thought no one could see? It was a fleeting thought, but I was glad it had occurred to me.

'Oh, love,' I began, putting down the sheet I'd been folding. 'Love, come on …'

He got to his feet and brushed the tears away with the heel of his hand. 'I'm fine,' he said, ignoring the arms I was holding out to him. 'I don't need you fussing. I'm fine on my own.'

'Okay,' I said, lowering them. I placed them on my hips instead. 'Okay. You want to talk?'

He stared at me. 'About what?'

I waved my arm in an arc. 'About what you were thinking when you did all this, maybe?'

'I wasn't thinking anything.'

'Because I think I know what I'd have been thinking. I'd have been thinking I hate the policemen, I hate Mike and I hate Casey. I hate Glenn. I hate John. I hate getting found out. I hate the world …'

He was inspecting a piece of puzzle, turning it over and over in his hand. I realised I had no idea what was going on in his head. Maybe he wasn't thinking anything of the sort.

'I don't care,' he said, his voice small. 'I don't care about nothing, no more. No one cares about me, an' I don't care about nothing.'

'Love, you know …' I faltered. Love, you know *what* exactly? '*I* care …' I started. 'I wouldn't do this if I didn't, would I? Nobody makes me take care of you, you know. I do it because I want to.'

'Well, you shouldn't do,' he said quietly. 'Cos I'm a wrecker.'

'A *what?*'

'That's what I'm good at.' He almost seemed to mentally regroup. To puff himself up now. He aimed the puzzle piece at the open box. 'I'm good at wrecking homes. My mum said. So you shouldn't.'

The jigsaw piece spun and hit its target.

Despite trying, I got nothing further from Spencer that day, and I opted not to keep teasing away at him. It was as if he'd flicked some sort of internal switch which created a force field around him, and meant that, though we could still communicate, it was only on a superficial level. He cleared his bedroom, he tidied, he vacuumed and he dusted. He was polite and contrite and all the things he'd always been so good at. And, sad though I was to admit that I felt that way about it, Monday and school couldn't come fast enough.

Besides, I had my own family to think about. It was Levi's third birthday and, having been so preoccupied with Spencer, I'd failed to do the thing I loved doing most in the world: to help Riley give him a Casey-style over-the-top party, just as I'd done for his mum and uncle Kieron for all their childhoods. I thought back to last year, when Levi had been two. We'd had two siblings with us then, Ashton and Olivia, both deeply damaged, and very demanding. But I'd still helped Riley organise a spectacular party: a full-on

*Teletubbies*-themed event, complete with costumes and scenery. It hardly seemed possible that I'd let an opportunity to do it all again slip by. It also felt terribly sad. You didn't get those special moments twice, after all, did you? It was a sure sign that I was letting things with Spencer get on top of me, because going to town with family celebrations was my 'thing', and I was famed for it.

But not this year. And I was touched by how adamant Riley seemed to be that, actually, she wasn't too disappointed, saying that now Levi was that bit bigger and, with a baby to look after, a big party would have been more than a little stressful. In fact she confided that she was actually a tiny bit relieved by my suggestion that we hold something lower-key, bless her; a small gathering in my conservatory, just for close family and a few friends from Levi's nursery, plus a couple of local lads I knew that Spencer had befriended. Though we didn't invite Chrissy, for obvious reasons.

We held it the following week, one day after school, and while Kieron's Lauren did the school run, and went and picked up Spencer, Riley and I enjoyed partying up my conservatory. And Kieron himself – who'd put himself in charge of the catering, bless him – did his last-minute creative tweaks to Levi's dinosaur cake.

And, small though it was, it all went like a dream. Spencer behaved impeccably, entertaining the little ones with his word-perfect Chipmunks karaoke, and for a while it was as if all was well in my world.

Which was perhaps what should have set alarm bells ringing. By six, my conservatory was liberally smeared and sprinkled with cake and crisp shards, and almost all of my guests had gone home. In fact I was just seeing the last out – a lovely little girl from Levi's nursery, plus her mum – when I saw a shape I recognised heading up our front path. It was our landlord, and straight away I could sense his embarrassment as he stepped aside to let the mum and her little one pass him.

'Is it all right if I come in, Casey?' he asked me. 'I could call back, if you like. You seem a little busy just now.'

'No, no,' I said, 'come in. You'll have to excuse all the mess, though. I've just held a party for little Levi – my grandson. There's only my brood left now. It's fine.'

But he still looked uncomfortable. 'Actually, I could do with speaking to you privately. If you don't mind, Casey. You know' – he nodded towards the conservatory – 'without the kids?'

By 'kids' he clearly meant mine – the grown-up ones. But why? What on earth was wrong? I couldn't imagine. But he was clearly anxious, which made me anxious, and the kids were leaving soon anyway. I popped my head round the door and explained I had some boring business with the landlord, and, thankfully, neither Riley nor Kieron seemed concerned. I think they were actually quite happy to have a reason not to stick around and do any more of the clearing up.

Within minutes I'd seen both my children and grand-children off, and Spencer, whose friends had left now and who looked as tired as I felt, seemed happy enough to slope off to the lounge and watch TV. And then my landlord, Mr Harris, dropped his bombshell.

'It's a petition,' he said, his voice faltering slightly as he gave it to me. I stared at it, trying to get my head around what he'd passed me. 'From all your neighbours,' he explained. 'About this latest kid you've been fostering. They've had enough is the bottom line,' he said. He cleared his throat, the way John did when he was the bearer of bad news. I felt for him suddenly. We'd known him for years, both as our current landlord – we'd lived in this house for a few years now – and before that as a neighbour, almost a friend. He knew all about our fostering, and had always spoken well of us. He obviously hated having to come here today. 'Well, as you can see. It's not been done lightly, this,' he added, echoing my thoughts, and seeming acutely uncomfortable in his role as messenger.

'But what does this mean?' I said, still unable to really take it in. Such a long list of signatures, next to carefully written addresses, some of which leapt out at me straight away.

'That they've had enough of him. That they no longer feel safe in their own houses. That they feel they can't let their kids play out any more. Things like that. Look,' he said, as the two of us stood there in the kitchen, the detritus of my happy afternoon piled all around us, 'it's just step one in a process, that's all.'

'Process? What process?' I asked. 'What do you mean?'

He gave me the sort of sympathetic look that actually does the opposite of its intention. This was serious, I suddenly realised. This wasn't just a list of disgruntled neighbours, complaining. These neighbours meant business. All the while Spencer was with us, they wanted us gone.

'Just step one,' Mr Harris said again, slowly. 'Of the process. Just a warning. We – or, rather the housing association, to be exact – can't, and don't want to, put you out of your home. Not at this stage. But you do need to know that this petition –'

'Is step one of the process,' I parroted back at him numbly. 'As you said.'

He shook his head sadly. 'I'm sure it's not going to come to that, Casey.'

'But it could.'

'Of course it *could*. We have a duty to *all* our tenants. As I'm sure you realise. My hands are tied here. We have a *duty*.'

But which, in the middle of everything, perhaps, we'd forgotten.

I saw him out, drew the blinds against the darkness, then finished cleaning. Then I counted the minutes until Mike arrived home.

# Chapter 21

Mike and I talked, long into the night. That our fostering would have such an effect on our local community was something that had never once occurred to us. But now it had, it suddenly seemed so understandable. There was no defence to be made, either. Spencer had caused no end of trouble, and with trouble came bad feeling, and now we knew the extent of it we both felt pretty awful.

It didn't help that we felt we'd let them all down so badly. Our neighbours had always been so supportive with our fostering. Always so quick to speak to us in the street or at the shops, asking how we were doing, and how were the kids settling in, etc. I felt both stupid and cross with myself that we hadn't realised this might happen – hadn't put enough thought into all this.

But our heart to heart extended further than Spencer. He'd be gone from us, at some point, and the problem would be over. But what about after that? What about other children we fostered? With our chosen speciality being to take on the challenging kids, the kids no one else would, there was every chance that, however many kids down the line it happened, we'd get another child like Spencer. Perhaps worse.

'We should move,' Mike announced, lying in bed in the wee hours. 'I mean, I know how much you love it here, but maybe it's an option we should consider. After all, with our own grown up and gone now … And you know what they say – a change is as good as a rest.'

We both laughed. Rests were never high on the agenda for either of us. If we wanted to rest, fostering would be the last thing we'd be doing. No, Mike was right. Much as I loved my home – particularly my beloved bolt-hole, my conservatory – it was something we *should* consider. And he made another good point. Many of the other foster carers we'd come across lived in simpler settings, often more rural, with plenty of outside space for kids to explore and less opportunity for getting into mischief – not to mention less density of neighbours to annoy. So, though I never saw us as the sort of people who'd live right out, on farms, keeping animals and growing veg, there was a lot to be said for getting a little bit more rustic.

We agreed I'd call Mr Harris first thing in the morning, and start looking for a new place to live. 'Not *too* far out, though,' I warned Mike before we went to sleep. 'We're not about to go all country bumpkin.'

My first job, however, was to write long apologetic letters to every single person on Mr Harris's list.

\* \* \*

Not that making the decision, for all my initial enthusiasm, didn't begin to weigh as heavy as the wintery weather. The reality of moving had other implications; we would probably – no, definitely – be moving further away from our children and our two beloved grandsons. It was one of those trade-offs that were so hard to deal with; we loved what we did, but how much were we prepared to sacrifice? I knew I wouldn't feel happy till I'd sat down and properly talked it through with Riley and Kieron. Though, for the moment, I had enough on my plate. By the middle of the following week, after what felt like days and days of heavy snowfall, the whole neighbourhood was all but snowed in. We were into December now and the heavens had really opened up. It was pointless trying to dig the car out with so much fresh snow falling, so Mike, like so many others, had taken to going to work on foot. And to complicate things further, Spencer's school had been closed since the weekend, as their heating had completely broken down.

But for all the hassle, it was at least an opportunity. With all the local kids in school, and the rest of the world occupied, it meant we could spend time together, just the two of us, which might just throw up an opportunity for him to open up to me. I was still at a loss to know how he was really coping with the knowledge that his family didn't want to see him any more. On the surface he only had the two modes of operation – either deny everything, as he'd done with the carrier bags of stuff, or, if caught red-handed, to break down and beg forgiveness and promise not to do it again. It was hopeless.

'Come on,' I said on the Thursday, when the snow had stopped falling. 'Let's walk to the park, shall we? We could have a snowball fight, if you like.'

'Yes!' said Spencer, punching the air excitedly and immediately dashing to and fro gathering hat, scarf and boots. And while he did so I had another thought, and went out to the shed, returning, after braving a possible run-in with big, hairy spiders, with my own booty.

'Oh, my God!' he yelped, clapping his hands together, eyes on stalks. 'Yessss! Oh, my God, you've got a sledge!'

I couldn't help but find his wonderful small-boy enthusiasm infectious. 'Indeed, I have,' I laughed, 'and if you play your cards right you can even sit and ride in it. C'mon, then. I'll pull you as far as the park.'

Spencer was in his element as he raced out onto the street and lowered himself into the blue plastic sledge. But though he whooped excitedly and we chatted and we laughed and had fun, in the end, for all my plans, we discussed nothing. Despite my best intentions, we had no meaningful or enlightening conversations. But, actually, that was okay. Better than okay, in fact, because our couple of hours in the park were some of the nicest we'd ever spent. We were wet and we were cold but we'd had such a glorious, exhilarating and uncomplicated time. We built a snowman and chased after one another pelting snowballs. All in all, just old-fashioned childish fun, really. And, trudging home, hand in hand, giggling and salivating over the prospect of getting our hands around mugs of hot chocolate, it occurred to me that we could be mistaken for any normal mother and son.

It was a bittersweet feeling, and when Spencer squeezed my hand tightly and looked up and smiled it was all I could do not to scoop him up and make him the promise that it would be okay, that I *did* care and that I'd never let him go.

Which surprised me. I was shocked at the strength of my emotions for this crazy, mixed-up kid, and, I realised, very afraid for his future.

But with more snow came more potential for my little oasis of calm to be buried in a fresh blizzard of aggro. By the end of the week the local schools had closed too, and the streets were full of excited youngsters building snowmen and playing games, and since Spencer had behaved so impeccably since the previous weekend I naturally had no choice but to let him out to play, however anxious I was about him annoying someone else.

And so he did, and after watching him for a while from my kitchen window I set about making a big beef stew and dumplings for tea. Just the thing in this weather, I thought, as I chopped veg, with the radio blaring Christmas songs beside me.

I let him have longer than his usual hour, as well, figuring that with the snow to keep him innocently occupied there was little likelihood of him getting up to mischief. How horribly wrong could I be?

By five, I called him in. He was wet through and shivering. But happy. 'Off upstairs,' I said, 'and straight out of those wet clothes. I've already run the bath so you can hop right on in. And you can change into your nightclothes when you're finished.'

'Have you?' he said, through chattering teeth. 'Thanks *so* much. That's wicked. Brrrr,' he finished, rubbing his hands together like a little old man. 'Just what I need. What's for tea?'

'Stew and dumplings,' I said, smiling as his eyes lit up further. He loved my stews. 'Now, get off up there. You're dripping on my carpet!'

Spencer trotting happily off upstairs, I then went back into the kitchen to pop the dumplings in the saucepan. Mike would be through the front door any minute, I calculated, which meant we could sit down to eat in half an hour.

And he did, right on cue, as I tidied the worktop. First I heard the door go and then the familiar sound of him banging his boots against the doorstep, to shake off the snow. But what I heard next was completely unfamiliar. To my consternation there seemed to be some sort of row starting up. I could hear male voices, several of them, raised and getting louder. Whatever was happening, they were clearly very angry.

I dashed into the hall to see Mike in the doorway, being confronted by three very angry-looking men. I felt a surge of fear – and compassion; I felt so sorry for my poor husband, standing on his own doorstep, in his stockinged feet. He looked so vulnerable. Yes, he was a big man, a tall one as well. But he'd be no match for three angry men.

They were all talking over one another, swearing and shouting, but one thing I did pick up was one of them saying, 'You either sort that fucking kid out, or we'll take it out on you!'

I came up behind Mike. 'You go back in the kitchen, love,' he told me.

'No way,' I said. 'I want to know what the hell is going on!'

Seeing me standing my ground seemed to have a calming effect. Either that or at least one of the mob on my doorstep had some old-fashioned values about kicking off and swearing in front of women. One of the men, at least, managed to calm down sufficiently to explain what it was that they were so furious about.

As night follows day, it was Spencer. He'd apparently been inserting big stones into snowballs, then throwing them at various neighbours' windows. Oh, God, I thought. Why? Why, why, why, why? And it seemed that, in one case, he'd done substantial damage, having shattered someone's living-room window. Which was bad enough in itself, but made immeasurably worse by the fact that the man's elderly mother had been sitting on the sofa at the time, and could so easily have been badly injured by the flying glass.

Thankfully the poor woman, though very shocked, was unharmed, but once again I had to stand, shame-faced, while Mike trotted out the usual story about Spencer, about how he was a troubled boy, in care, and only with us temporarily, and how we'd of course pay for the replacement of the broken window. There was very little else we could do.

As we turned to go back in, we both saw Spencer on the stairs. He was halfway down them, wrapped in a towel, shivering and looking terrified, obviously drawn down by the sound of the commotion.

'Get back upstairs,' I said, glaring at him. I was so angry and upset by all the aggression on the doorstep that by now I was shaking. 'Go back upstairs, get your pyjamas on,' I snapped. 'And then come straight down for your tea.'

He did as I asked, without comment, and I went and joined Mike in the kitchen. He was leaning his hands against the sink, staring out into the night sky. It was so unfair. He really didn't need to come home to all this after a hard day at work.

I went and checked the stew, then started laying the table.

'I'm so sorry, love,' I said. 'This just isn't on. And I don't know about you, but I really can't face having yet another mealtime ruined ...'

He turned around. 'You're absolutely right, love. He'll start babbling on about his innocence and how one of his friends did it, and we'll get absolutely nowhere apart from halfway up the bloody wall. No, you're right. We'll make it clear. No discussion. End of subject. Deal with it tomorrow, yes? Speak to John ... Honestly,' he finished, 'this is getting out of hand now. I'm bloody fuming. I thought that guy was going to get stuck in, I really did.'

Spencer, however, seemed to have no intention of doing likewise. I dished out the tea, put his plate in front of him, and Mike made it clear as I did so that, yes, he was in trouble for throwing his stone-encrusted snowballs, and yes, that was what the men had come about, but that, no, we weren't interested in what he had to say about it. We'd deal with it tomorrow once we'd spoken to John about what the consequences might be. And through all this, Spencer said nothing. He just hung his head, looked contrite and nodded where appropriate, realising that to argue his point would be fruitless. Or so I thought. It was to turn out that his quiet, appeasing stance might have been much more to do with a sense of relief about having not been caught out doing *much* worse.

'I'll come round and take him off out for swimming and lunch, then.' It was a couple of days later and, following my latest chat with John, this was Penny on the phone. Despite the threatened cutbacks, and the fact that Penny had been taken off 'Spencer duties' for the time being, John had felt that this new development warranted bringing her back in for a few extra hours.

And though Penny taking Spencer off on one of her outings felt to me a little bit like he was being rewarded for his bad behaviours, rather than punished, I wasn't arguing. Who knew? Maybe one of John's main motivations was to give me a little breathing space as well. Which was very welcome. With his school still closed and the roads still too treacherous for driving, I was beginning to feel less like Spencer's jailor, and more like we were doing time together. All my warm maternal feeling from the week before was melting fast. Perhaps he was right. Perhaps he was so good at being a 'wrecker', as he called it, that to try to do anything to set him on the right path *was* pointless. Maybe I should just stop my 'fussing' and let him get on with it.

'That'll be great,' I said, feeling guilty for mentally cheering. But I was at my wits' end and I knew I really needed the break.

I decided, once they'd gone, that after I'd done my housework I'd walk round to Riley's. Suddenly, I really didn't want to stay in my own house. It might have just been a reaction to being snowed in, of course – after all, not being able to jump in my car and go to town was definitely losing its novelty. For one thing, it would soon be Christmas and, despite a bout of internet shopping, I didn't feel I'd had a chance to prepare anything yet. By this time I had usually put up my tree and decorations, and would normally be hugging myself with excitement every time I thought about it, and looking forward, with the same sort of thrill as a child, to the upcoming family celebrations. But as for this year … It seemed all wrong to want to escape. I'd always been so happy and house proud. And now my beloved home really did feel like a prison; a place – and a neighbourhood – I wanted to flee from.

I'd been so worried about Riley's reaction to us moving, but when I'd called to talk it through she'd been incredibly supportive. 'Mum,' she'd said, 'do it! It's a brilliant idea. A fresh start, a nicer area … what's not to like?' I loved her youthful lack of sentimentality, and hoped I'd soon feel likewise. But best of all was that she added that if we did move some distance then she and David would simply do likewise.

'Really?' I'd said.

'Of course,' she laughed. 'You think I'd lose my free childcare? No, seriously,' she went on, 'we've been thinking about moving out a bit anyway. Levi will be school age before you know it and we want to live somewhere where there's nice schools.'

But the cheerful spirit that accompanied my chilly trot around to my daughter's was to be dissipated only an hour after I arrived there.

It was Penny, calling my mobile, and immediately apologising for being 'about to completely ruin' my day. She then went on to explain why that was.

They'd been swimming, apparently, but it still being too early for lunch they'd made a detour to the large department store in town, as she wanted to pick up a few bits. Spencer, she told me, had been somewhat reluctant about going in and, half an hour later, it became obvious why. She was calling me, she told me, from the store manager's office, the two of them having been accosted by a store detective about a bout of shoplifting Spencer had indulged in the previous week. And there was no question of him wheedling his way out of it either, as they had it all on CCTV.

'So could you head home, d'you think?' she asked. 'Because they've called the police, and the plan is, once they've dealt with matters here, for us all to meet up together at your house.'

My day ruined, I put the phone down and promptly burst into tears. Was there no end to this child's criminal activity? How had he done all this? *When* had he done all this? I could only imagine that in his one hour of daily freedom he had managed to run the five minutes into town, with me believing that he was playing with Aaron on the next street. Hard as it was to believe, they had the evidence, so he must have. Was he some kind of impulsive kleptomaniac, as well? I brokenly and clumsily tried to explain things to Riley, and having done so regretted it – she was livid.

'Enough!' she said. 'Mum, you cannot go on like this. There are jobs and there are jobs, and I know you love yours, but I can't bear to see you and Dad suffering all this. God, while his parents' – she literally spat out the word 'parents' – 'just swan off and wash their hands of him. It's wicked!' She paused for breath, and snatched a tissue up. I duly blew my nose. 'And it's not just that,' she went on. 'This kid is clearly not normal, so he obviously needs some other sort of intervention, some sort of professional help that you and Dad aren't qualified to provide. It's not fair on either of you and it's not fair on Spencer. They need to *do* something!'

'They are trying …'

'Then they need to try harder. I will not have my mother put through this all the time.'

It took a good 15 minutes to calm Riley down and convince her that I was okay now. Then I trudged home again, actually grateful for the cold, crisp winter air, and called Mike on my mobile to fill him in. He'd been on an early shift anyway, so said he'd be home, and in fact cheered me no end by beating me to it, and brandishing a hot coffee on the doorstep.

But caffeine alone, I decided, wouldn't be enough, so I also broke out my pack of emergency cigarettes – about which Mike, bless his heart, never so much as made a murmur.

Within ten minutes the latest posse were all assembled. If there was one constant in our lives as foster carers, it was this: that they would be punctuated regularly by meetings with people. The cast would change – social workers, policemen, care professionals – but the event itself, actually, didn't much. Hot beverages and biscuits, grim expressions and manila folders. And today's was to prove no exception. Today's attendees – Mike and me, Spencer, two police officers, Penny – gathered round the dining table at which the star of the show was a particularly arresting-looking manila folder.

But not nearly as arresting as the information it contained. For the police weren't just here to discuss Spencer's department-store thieving, they had a whole host of other misdemeanours on their minds.

I listened numbly as one of the officers, a pretty, smiley blonde woman, explained that there were a number of unsolved crimes in the area and that, in almost every instance, the perpetrator fitted Spencer's description.

I looked across at him, then, expecting tears, the whole denial show, but it was as if there'd been some shift in how he decided to view the world now, because as the eye-boggling list went on – burglary, attempted arson, criminal damage, theft of a mini-moto motorbike – he wore an expression that was something akin to pride. Even Penny, with her long experience of counselling deeply damaged children, was beginning to look as pale as the snow outside. And, as ever, I knew we were all thinking the same thing: that this 'perp' was an eight-year-old child. As one of the officers later noted, there was 'going off the rails' and there was 'being completely off the flippin' sat nav!' This little boy could not have been a more authentic version of a street kid if he'd been born in the slums of Bogotà.

The meeting went on for well over an hour. And after Penny left, the police officers made a strange request. What they wanted to do, with our permission, was to take Spencer and Mike out in a patrol car with them the following morning, and have him point out as they drove all the places he'd committed crimes. It was a request he acceded to almost happily. And I wondered, as we saw them out, having agreed they'd be back the next day at 11, about a book my children had loved, called *There's No Such Thing as a Dragon*. In the book, the little boy finds a dragon under his bed, but the grown-ups he confides in tell him dragons don't exist. Of course, the book has a message about listening to children, because each time someone says, 'There's no such thing as a dragon,' the dragon grows a little bit bigger, so that, in the end, they all *have* to notice him.

And pay him some attention, of course. Was this key to all of Spencer's behaviour? I'll get worse and I'll get worse and I'll get worse, till you notice? Was that his goal, on some level? Just to be noticed? Because he seemed almost euphoric when I sent him off to watch some TV.

But the day wasn't done with surprises. The meeting over, the thing I most needed to do was call John. These new revelations were serious indeed, and social services would need to be informed. I went into the hall and grabbed the house phone to ring him, taking it with me into the kitchen.

John answered after only one ring.

'Ah, Casey,' he said. 'Thanks for getting back to me so quickly –'

'Getting back? Did you call me, then?'

'Yes, on your mobile.'

'Oh, I see. I didn't have it with me. We've been holed up in a meeting, so …'

'Well, pin your ears back, because have I got news for you.'

'News? What kind of news? Small news? Big, big news? Good news, I hope, because …'

'Oh, extremely good, potentially. Not that we should jump the gun because it all sounds a bit incredible, but …'

'What?'

'Kerry Herrington. Spencer's mum. She's left her husband.'

I took this fact in, and considered it, and having done so didn't find it quite as exciting as John clearly did. If she'd struck me as anything it was definitely as the sort of mother who'd at some point perhaps walk out on her kids. I said so.

'No, no, it's not like that,' he corrected. 'Quite the opposite. She has left him and taken the rest of the kids *with* her. And the reason she's been in touch with us – well, with Glenn – is to find out how to get Spencer back!'

'You're kidding.'

'I'm not. But there's much more to tell, and I'd rather not do it over the phone. Is there a time I could pop by, when Spencer won't be around? It's obviously imperative he knows nothing about this …'

'How does 11 a.m. tomorrow grab you?'

I honestly didn't know what to think when I put the phone down.

# Chapter 22

The following morning, after having had almost no sleep at all, I found myself down in the kitchen by 7 a.m., almost unheard of on a weekend. But then again, I told myself as I turned up the heating, every day had seemed like a week-end day just recently. I prayed that the schools would soon be re-opened, and I also prayed that whatever John had to tell me would be something, *anything*, to cheer me up a bit. I had been tossing and turning all night. Though Spencer, oblivious, had fallen asleep at 6 p.m., Mike and I had been discussing the latest turn of events for most of the night, attempting hundreds of guesses as to what could possibly be happening, none of which felt faintly plausible. Her leave *him*? And taking the kids? It just seemed so unlikely. If John had said it was the other way around, then perhaps. I couldn't wait for the clock to creep round to 11.

Spencer came down just after Mike, at nine o'clock and, as I suspected, he was now in a more sombre mood. His cocky attitude when his long list of crimes was being totted up had been replaced with a look of deep concentration. 'How long before the cops come, Mike?' he asked over his breakfast.

Mike stared at him for a moment before replying, quite pointedly, 'The *police* will be here at 11, Spencer. And if I were you, after breakfast I'd go and sit down quietly and make some kind of list. A reminder of things you need to tell them when they get here. It'll look better on you.' He paused. 'If that's possible.'

Spencer did. He got dressed and then sat quietly at the dining table with a pencil and a sheet of paper, carefully making his 'list'. I sighed as I went up to get ready before they left. He looked just like a child who might have been carefully thinking about what to ask Santa for on his Christmas list – deep in thought, chewing the end of his pencil, and leaning forward to scribble when hit by a flash of inspiration. If only, I thought, as I went up the stairs, that *was* what he was doing.

In the end, it was 11 a.m. when John arrived. Having seen off Mike, the police and the diminutive felon, I opened the front door again, sending yet another swirl of freezing air to eddy round my ankles. The snow was falling more thickly now, and Spencer and Mike's footprints had already disappeared. John, who'd obviously had to park around the corner as so many cars were snowed in on our road now, looked just about as cold as I felt. 'Come on, come straight into the conservatory,' I told him. 'I've already brewed a pot of coffee. And I've got the heater going hell for leather. You'll soon be toasty.'

'That sounds wonderful,' he said, following me in, rubbing his hands together. 'And I hope it's not a problem for you, me coming round on a Sunday. I just thought we ought to crack on with this really. What with Christmas coming, and things needing to be put in place and so on …'

I poured out two coffees while he shrugged his arms out of his coat. 'Listen to you,' I admonished. 'You're the one turning out to go to work on a Sunday.'

'Well, needs must,' he said, as I handed his mug to him. He curled his hands around it gratefully. 'How long d'you think they'll be gone?' he asked. 'Because, boy, have I a story to tell *you* …'

I had no idea what to expect, I realised, as we settled down on the two sofas in the pleasingly warm conservatory. The only news I had so far was the one thing he'd already told me: that Kerry had left Danny and that she'd been on to social services to enquire about how she could go about getting Spencer back. Which had been something of an astonishing development in itself, but tantalisingly light on all the details.

But John, it seemed, was now about to supply them.

'So,' he said, 'this is the position. She and the younger two children – the older ones are with their auntie, but we'll come to that in a bit – are currently staying at a battered women's refuge, about half an hour from here. You probably know it, Rebecca House?'

I nodded, taking it in. 'Okaaaayyy …'

'They left in something of a moonlight flit, by all accounts, aided by her sister.'

'That's the auntie, then?'

'Yup,' he answered. 'Couple of years older than Kerry. Been living in Spain for the last decade, by all accounts. Never had kids, recently divorced. But I'll come to her in a minute. Better if I start at the beginning, don't you think?'

I nodded. 'Go on, then. I'm all ears.'

And it turned out to be quite a story. I'd been doing what I do long enough to have seen a few things, but what John began telling me – if it was true, at least, and John seemed completely sure it was – then it made for some pretty depressing telling. It also made me realise that however switched on you thought you were about people, in some cases you really should not assume anything – not if you didn't want it turned on its head. And the first shock was one that I'd never have guessed. Spencer's dad – the one he so idolised – wasn't actually Spencer's dad at all.

Spencer's mother had married Danny Herrington very young. The younger of two daughters, with an absent father and an alcoholic mother, now deceased, Kerry had been a little like a lamb to the slaughter. Perhaps desperate to escape, and for a life that felt more secure than one she'd so far lived, she got married at just 18 – to this capable, charming, man who seemed so keen to take care of her – and had her first two children with him very quickly. But it soon became apparent that behind closed doors things were going badly wrong. Though to the outside world Danny was affable and popular, at home he was increasingly violent and controlling. He wouldn't allow his wife to go out anywhere without him, to see friends, or even family, and she gradually grew more and more terrified of crossing him. At that time, though Kerry's mum was in a residential home some way away, her sister didn't live too far off, so there was at least that family connection. But once the sister moved abroad – she went to Spain with her husband's job, apparently – there was nothing in the way of family nearby and Kerry became more and more isolated.

'And turned to the bottle, like her mother?' I asked John. I knew this sort of tendency often ran in families, whether through genes or through upbringing, perhaps both. But John shook his head. 'Apparently not,' he said. 'Not yet. Though with two small children to bring up, and him not earning much, they did start to struggle financially. It was then that he realised they couldn't manage on his wages, and grudgingly allowed her to take a part-time job. And that's when the trouble really started.'

John explained that Kerry had got a job in a local garage, doing bookkeeping and general admin, for a few hours a week. She was in her early twenties by then – her prime – and about six months into this she met a man – a new mechanic there – and began an affair. 'So what do you think happened?' John asked me, pausing to sip his coffee.

It didn't take a great deal of thinking, after what he'd told me. 'She fell pregnant?' I answered.

John nodded. 'Exactly.'

'With Spencer?'

'With Spencer. By now she'd been seeing this guy for several months, by all accounts. He was a divorcee, no kids, early thirties, and of course she saw this as her chance to escape. So while hubby was at work one day she packed up all her stuff, hers *and* the children's – I think one might have started school by now, but that doesn't matter – and took them round to the home of her boyfriend.

'But it wasn't to be. Call her naïve – I think I probably would, but perhaps that's understandable – but she'd really thought that when she explained she was pregnant with his child he'd scoop her up, take care of them all, the whole hearts and flowers thing –'

'John,' I interrupted, 'you're sounding horribly cynical.'

'Forgive me,' he said, shaking his head ruefully. 'I know I shouldn't. But when you see how many kids' lives are blighted in the aftermath of this sort of adult mess …'

'Fair point,' I agreed. Poor Spencer. *Poor* Spencer.

'Sorry,' John said, grinning. 'Off on my soapbox! Anyway, yes, the guy, of course, was having none of it. Was horrified. Made it clear that he had no interest in taking on her kids, or her having a baby, for that matter. No interest in *her* either, except on one condition: that she left the kids with their father and had an abortion. Otherwise, no go. He was planning to move away, and did shortly after, apparently. Probably couldn't run fast enough.'

'So she went back to Danny?'

'Not exactly. The boyfriend had at least let her stay at his place till she could work out what to do – I think at that time she'd had this plan that she might take the kids to Spain, to be near her sister. Though as far as having the cash, or the courage, or even the wherewithal … Anyway, while she was busy vacillating, Danny tracked her down and, like the boyfriend, he had his own plan of action in place. Soon as he knew she was pregnant, he said pretty much the same. Either she had an abortion and she and the children came back to him, or it was simple. He'd go to court and, given the history – her affair, her unstable upbringing, her general fecklessness, etc. – he'd make sure she didn't see her children again.'

'But he couldn't have pulled that off, surely? Why would the courts have awarded him custody?'

'Oh, they could have, and, from what Kerry's sister says, they probably would have. Could have charmed the birds out of the trees, by all accounts. She was pretty frank about it all. For a long time she refused to believe her own sister about him. This was a man, by all accounts, that was a very popular guy. And, well, you've met the couple, haven't you? What conclusions did you and Mike draw?'

I shook my head and groaned. 'Point taken …'

'*Exactly*. Me too. Anyway, by now of course it was too late to *have* an abortion, because Kerry had kept everything quiet for so long. Which left her effectively homeless and penniless, with two children and also pregnant. So she did what she thought was the only thing she *could* do. She went back to him, with her tail between her legs.'

'And then had Spencer.'

'Indeed. And of course another rule was put in place: that no one must ever know that Spencer wasn't Danny's. Happy families and all that. His pride and his reputation kept in place.'

It beggared belief. 'I just don't see it,' I told John, still astonished. 'It just seems so at odds with the mild-mannered man we've met. He always seems so concerned, and so polite, holding it together.'

'Oh, don't be fooled,' said John. 'I'm now beginning to see the bigger picture. Now we've spoken properly to the sister – and seen some of the evidence, for that matter – it's all begun falling into place. That boy no more put himself in care than flew to Acapulco. I wouldn't be surprised to hear Danny Herrington had been scheming how to get rid of him for years. Cuckoo in the nest, wasn't he?' John smiled, but without mirth. 'You know what the psychologist said about Spencer probably being a sociopath? Well, there's your sociopath. That man. Right there.'

I tried to take this in – comparing the man I'd met and the picture John had painted, with the psychologist's words about how sociopaths could mimic normal emotions, and behave as people expected them to, clamouring for attention in my brain. 'But it's all so unexpected. I mean Kerry, from what I've seen, is really in no state to –'

'It's down to the sister. She got divorced and she's now back in Britain. And she's tenacious – you'll probably meet her, and then you'll see – and she didn't like what she saw. Started with some bruises, apparently.' He made a motion with one hand on his other forearm. 'Bruises on Kerry that she didn't like the look of, and which Kerry couldn't – or wouldn't – explain. Plus the state she was in, of course, the heavy drinking – lots of experience of that, of course, and also – in fact mainly – the fact that Spencer had been taken away by social services. She was – still is – the only other person who knows he's not Danny's. So, as you can imagine, she wasn't going to let it rest. And eventually it all came out – the whole sorry mess of it, and how he's been paying back that poor woman – and her love-child, poor innocent little Spencer – since pretty much the day he was born.'

'And she went on to have two more with him ...' I mused.

'I know. Grim, isn't it?' And John grimaced himself at this point. 'Perhaps not in much of a position to refuse him.'

'"To do *anything* about him,' I said, as it hit me. 'How could she? She must have been living through a nightmare. Because if she had tried to take him on she probably *would* have lost her kids. Either to him, through the courts, or ending up with them in care. God, you just never know, do you?'

And suddenly everything began falling into place: Spencer trying to explain how he was his dad's favourite but that he had to 'act bad' to show he wasn't. Did his mother tell Spencer that? It suddenly seemed so clear she must have. How she'd done that deal with him about how if he promised to be good social services would let him come home again. I thought back to the day when he 'threw a brick at his sibling'. His mother hadn't seen that. Danny had *told* her he'd done it. And like a robot she'd done what she was probably programmed to do – do as she was told. Give her poor child merry hell. What would have been the consequences of her showing him affection? A beating from her husband? It made me shudder. And, worse, in her befuddled state, had she come to despise him too? For all the pain his very existence had caused her.

The more I thought, the grimmer were my thoughts about Spencer, treated like an outcast in his own home by his own parents. No wonder Spencer had turned out the way he had. Not the devil's spawn – just the product of an ill-starred affair. For which he had paid a brutally heavy price.

'So what's happening now, then?' I asked John, my own coffee mug still half-full, but cold.

John cleared his throat again. 'What's happening is that she wants her son back. Though, knowing what we now know, it's obviously not that straightforward. She has the younger two with her at the refuge, and her sister is fostering the older two – the nine- and ten-year-olds – while a plan of action's drawn up. She'll be housed, of course, but almost everything depends on her actually following through on the charges she's brought against her husband –'

'He's let that happen, then? Let her take the children? Does he know where they are?'

'Didn't have a lot of choice in the matter, really. He's been charged with one assault – and there are more charges to follow – and Kerry has taken out an injunction against him. This means he can't go anywhere near her or he'll be charged further, obviously, but as for the kids, social services have taken precautionary measures. All four of them are now classed as 'at risk', and for the time being at least Danny has been told that he can't have contact. Not while all this is going on, anyway. He'll need to put in his own applications for contact via a solicitor and the courts, presumably.

'But you know the score, Casey. How many times do we see these things *not* being followed through? Which is why, as of right now, Spencer mustn't know *anything*. Mustn't even have an inkling. I know you'd love to be able to give him something positive to cling on to, but if it falls through … Because the whole thing's still a pretty big ask. But I'm hopeful. So far she's been true to her word on the drinking – joined AA, and that – and I'm told she's equally determined about Spencer. And I believe her. So if she can crack it, there's light at the end of the tunnel. A tiny glimmer of light, anyway. Let's just hope things haven't gone too far.'

I spent a while after John had gone, sitting at my laptop, and going through my journal, thinking about Spencer's anger towards his mother, his lack of empathy, his compulsive need to do bad things, his streak of cruelty. Would the psychologist who'd seen him have come to a different conclusion if he'd known everything I knew now? No wonder Spencer had such enormous issues to deal with. He'd been paying for having had the misfortune to be born from the day he'd arrived on the planet. How did you process a reality in which your father routinely mistreated you and showed his hate for you (that bruising he'd first appeared with at social services with, for instance?), while your mum – the one person in the world you should be able to rely on – just stood there and let it happen, because she was too busy drinking away her own pain, too afraid to do anything and, perhaps, regretting the day she'd given birth to him?

That, I thought grimly, as I shut down the computer, was an altogether much bigger ask.

# Chapter 23

I was fit to burst by the time Spencer had gone to bed that evening and I was at last able to fill Mike in properly. He was as gobsmacked as I was – it was such a lot to take in. Not to mention being so at odds with everything about the family we'd so far seen and been told. No wonder, we kept repeating to each other. No wonder. The poor child. What a grim hand of cards he'd started life with. We agreed we almost didn't want to allow ourselves to hope. If there was a chance of it working out, then that would be the best news imaginable, but given the number of damaged – and damaging – people in this equation, it still felt much more likely that in the end nothing would come of this news. Spencer's mother, even if she had the best of intentions, would probably be too far gone to deal with her own demons, and now that Danny Herrington had been flagged up as the villain of the piece, and the other children classi-fied as at risk, the outcome might actually be little different for Spencer. The only difference, we speculated grimly, might be that it was no longer just Spencer coming into the hands of social services. With the entire family blown apart, it might be that all the children ended up in care.

But it was important we get back to the business at hand, which was the fact of Spencer's crime spree and the consequences it would have for him. Which in the short term, the police had decided, following their outing, would be for him to pay a visit to the station to be formally interviewed and charged. That such a thing could happen to so young a child appalled me. And now I knew what I knew, I felt zealously protective towards him. Mike, however, took a different view.

'I'm going to take a half-day off work,' he decided, 'so that it's *me* that goes with him. If it's me rather than you, it'll seem that much more serious. And if you stay at home, too, even more so. Because that's what this is about, love: putting the fear of ruddy God into him. That's all they really want to do. It'll all seem very official, but I doubt they're going to actually do anything. Just hopefully put him right off the idea of a life of crime.'

Come Monday morning, therefore, it was Mike who took charge once again, and all I could do was stay at home and fret about what might be happening. And when the post came, and with it our first clutch of Christmas cards, I realised that the festivities couldn't have been further from our minds. Instead, it felt like our whole lives were in limbo. We knew all this stuff about Spencer's family, which we could do nothing with – we couldn't even *tell* him – we had the ongoing business with the police to contend with, and where normally our own family lives would be the one reassuring constant, right now we were contemplating moving out of our home. It was all horribly disorientating, and I hated it.

But on the plus side, the post had also brought a letter from the letting agents, containing details of a couple of properties to rent that might suit us. And as I looked at all the details, I felt my spirits slowly lifting. One of the properties, a four-bedroom semi, was only about three miles from our current home. It was in a much quieter, leafy area, in a good part of town, and right outside it was a huge grassy designated children's play area and, at the edge of that, even a couple of small shops. It also had a really big garden, with mature trees and shrubs, so it was both private and would go a long way towards settling my anxiety about leaving my beloved blossom tree behind.

As I'd expected, my mood was dampened slightly on Mike and Spencer's return. And as Mike explained the situation, it all sounded very serious. Because of the scale of Spencer's wrongdoing, it had been decided to skip the usual stages of warning and reprimand, and instead to go to the final stage in the process. He'd actually been formally charged, and with a whopping 23 different offences. And, as Mike announced, with great gravity, released on bail.

I was stunned, but, to my relief, once Spencer went out for his precious hour of peer time in the snow, Mike explained that the consequences weren't going to be as grim as I'd first feared. All that would happen, in all likelihood, would be that Spencer would be asked to have a couple of sessions with the youth-offending officer. Even so, this was something almost unheard of for a child this age, and we could only hope that these measures – put in place for that very reason – would go some way to minimising the risk of Spencer embarking on a life of crime.

The visit to the station had thrown up another development. Spencer hadn't just been compulsively stealing, as a response to his distress. He'd actually been stealing to order, for a local fence – a teenage boy who, we were both dismayed to learn, lived on our very own street. And Spencer had apparently had no compunction about spilling beans and naming names. 'He told the police everything,' Mike recounted to me. 'Almost proudly, as well. Literally *everything*: orders taken, goods delivered, payments made, and when the officer asked him what sort of payment he got for various things, it really hit home to me. "Oh, it depended on the gear," he goes. "If it was just like toolboxes 'n' stuff, I got a toy car or summat, but if it was really good stuff, like jewels or computer games, sometimes I got a pound!" Honest, Casey, it beggars belief.'

It was almost comic. Darkly comic, and once again I thought of Dickens, and Fagin, and how much this image of Spencer, running around doing his thieving to order, conjured up the image of a modern-day Artful Dodger. But it was *too* dark. This was the reality of how easily a small child could be exploited and criminalised if left to fall prey to the sort of gangs that ran the streets.

The very streets we *lived* on, in fact. I smiled ruefully to myself. It seemed that every day brought fresh evidence that this house move would be no bad thing at all. And if we wanted evidence that it would definitely be no bad thing for Spencer, we were to get it, only ten minutes later.

We were still discussing the Herringtons, and how completely we'd been drawn into thinking of Danny Herrington as being Spencer's guardian angel when he was, in fact, his nemesis, when the doorbell rang. I reacted as I always did these days, by feeling a knot form immediately in my stomach. But it wasn't a disgruntled neighbour; it was one of the local children, a girl of about nine from further up the road.

'Spencer's already out, love,' I explained, pointing. 'Over there, with the others.'

'I know,' she said, with the sort of officiousness that girls her age were good at. 'I just came to tell you he's scaring all the little ones. He's got some police letter an' he's telling them all they might go to jail.'

'What?' I said, rolling my eyes. Then the penny dropped. The little so and so must have managed to somehow sneak out his charge sheet, and was obviously now bragging about it amongst his friends. With the girl at my side I marched across to the huddle of kids across the street. 'Spencer!' I snapped crossly. 'You know exactly what I'm here for. That charge sheet. And you, as well. Play time over. Inside NOW!'

So much for Mike thinking he'd be all contrite and anxious, I thought angrily, as I frogmarched him back across the street. So much for the gravity of the situation sinking in, either. I got him inside and let him have both barrels. Sometimes an old-fashioned bawling out was exactly what was needed even if, generally, I didn't hold with too much shouting.

'You just never learn, do you?' I yelled at him. I couldn't help it. 'Only back from the police station for five minutes and you're already out there thinking you're something clever. What is it going to take for you to realise you're in trouble? What is it going to take for you to realise you're headed nowhere? Being a scummy, no-good criminal, who preys on nice, decent people, is not big and not remotely clever, you understand? It's pathetic. It's for fools and for idiots and morons! Do you want to *completely* wreck your life, is that it? Is that the plan here?' I had my hands on his shoulders and had bent slightly, to be at eye level. 'Answer me!' I snapped again, my temper truly lost now. 'IS it?'

I probably realised just what I'd said to him the same minute he did. And I could have kicked myself. How could he *not* wreck his life, as things stood? Because that was what he was best at. Being a wrecker. Hadn't his mother already made that abundantly clear?

I watched the hard lines on his face soften into the crumples of imminent tears. And in that instant I realised that this simple encounter – his wrongdoing, my anger, this heated dressing down, the telling off – was such a staple of every childhood, because that's how kids learned. But it was one, I suspected, that Spencer had completely lacked. Hadn't he spent all his time wandering the streets, unchecked? He'd spoken the truth before. No one had ever really cared about him – certainly not enough to try and keep him on the right track.

'I don't know,' he said suddenly, but less in anger than in anguish. 'I don't know why I do stuff I do. I just *do*!'

The tears plopped from his eyes and I gathered him in towards me. 'I don't want to be me any more, Casey. I *hate* me,' he sobbed. 'I'm sick of bein' the devil's prawn! I want to stop. I don't wanna *be* that. I just want my mum and dad to want me back.'

'It's all right,' I soothed. 'It's all right …'

'But it's not,' he said, pulling back to look at me. His whole body, I realised, was shaking now. 'It's not fair! If they got too many kids, why can't they get rid of one of the other ones now, and have ME back. Why? Why, Casey? WHY?'

It was obviously something that had preyed on his young mind from day one. And why wouldn't it have? It must have been torture. *Why* him? What had *he* done? Why had he been singled out?

It was the biggest job imaginable not to be able to share what I knew with him. But not impossible, chiefly because I was still all too aware that, in terms of his future, it might still count for very little.

I was aware of Mike now, who'd obviously been standing in the doorway, hands in pockets. And knew he was thinking the same thing as me.

But I had to find something positive to get out of this situation, and, racking my brains as I hugged him and tried to calm him, I hit upon an idea: write some letters. I'd been here before, with so many children. Sit them down, give them space and help to order their thoughts, and have them put pen to paper. And old-fashioned process, but one that always seemed to help. And as experience had also shown me, it was help that could prove vital. Kids in this sort of emotional turmoil, reaching crisis point, as Spencer was, were actually in a very serious place. Their heads full of tangled thoughts, which they had no means to process, let alone try to explain to anyone, they could so easily, and catastrophically, implode. That was the real danger, and I was all too aware that, for Spencer, that place might soon be reached.

'I know,' I soothed again, 'and I would be asking that myself, love. But you know what? One good way to start to make you feel better would be if you wrote to some of the people you stole from. Or anyone, really,' I ventured. 'Anyone you think you might have things to say to. How about we do that, hmm? Sit down together and you get some things off your chest? We don't have to post them to people if you don't want to, but sometimes just saying sorry – getting it all down on paper – is a really good way to start making you feel better.'

He was acquiescent now and, nodding glumly, allowed me to lead him to the kitchen table, and after Mike had gathered together a couple of pens and a pad of paper, he let me prompt him to draw up a short list of the people he felt he most had to apologise to.

His words were heartbreakingly simple to read, and he used a form of them for almost every letter he wrote out: *I am sorry for all the trouble I caused you and I hope you feel better soon. Love from Spencer Herrington, the boy in care at number 57.*

And he was adamant he did want to deliver them, as well, so once they were done Mike managed to find a pack of envelopes and, one by one, the letters were carefully folded and inserted, ready for us to deliver around the neighbourhood after tea.

And now he seemed calmer, I had another idea. 'Tell you what,' I said, once the last envelope had been sealed, 'since you're at the table with pen and paper, how about Mike goes and fetches the Argos catalogue and we make a start on your Christmas list as well?'

It was as if someone had pulled a cord and switched a light on inside his head. His smile – a genuine smile of astonishment and joy – could have lit up the whole neighbourhood, fences and all. Had he ever in his life known the simple childish pleasure of wanting something and knowing there was someone in the world who genuinely wanted to get it for you? But it seemed he wasn't quite done with his letter writing yet.

'That would be brill,' he said, 'but can I do one more letter first, for my mum?'

'Of *course*,' I said, feeling a wave of satisfaction wash over me. Whatever came next, this could only be a good thing.

So we sat for ten minutes more while, asking here and there for help with spelling, Spencer sat and wrote the saddest little letter I had ever seen.

*Dear Mum*, it read, *I am so sorry for my life. I never meant to hurt you and I love you with a big heart. I want you to kiss me when my dad isn't looking so he doesn't think I'm a girl's blouse, I promise I'll let you kiss me. Casey and Mike are fixing me into a proper good kid like our Lewis. When can I come home, Mum? Love for ever and ever, Spencer xxxxxxxxxxxxxxxxxxxxxxxxxx*

He filled every spare bit of white paper with kisses, and

when it came to putting it in an envelope he looked up at me. 'You gotta make sure she only gets it in secret, though,' he told me. I had to turn away, then, so he wouldn't see my own tears. Mike, having stood behind him and read it as well, had already had to leave the room.

I leaned down and kissed the top of Spencer's head. 'Absolutely,' I said. 'Glenn will be able to organise that, I promise.' And it was thankfully a promise I knew I could keep. I couldn't help feeling slightly antagonistic towards Kerry, though. Spencer knew nothing, and I guessed what he didn't know couldn't hurt him, but, by God, I'd feel so angry if now she'd come as far as she had she failed to come through for her son.

Mike returned with the Argos catalogue and, happily, the mood swiftly changed. Like any other boy of Spencer's age, he duly obliged and, regardless of cost, merrily ticked off pretty much everything in the section of boys' toys, while I set about rummaging in my fridge and freezer, trying to decide what to have for tea.

'You know what?' Mike said, having sat and flicked through the TV listings while Spencer compiled his list. 'It says here that *The Wizard of Oz* is on later. How about we forget proper tea, make a big load of popcorn, grab some chocolates and sweets – it'll only take me a minute to pop to the corner shop if we need stuff – make some milkshakes and watch a Christmas movie?'

This galvanised Spencer. 'Yay!' he cheered. 'Yay! C'mon, Casey. Let's all go wild for a change. Throw the veg in the bin!' he then commanded, making both Mike and me roar with laughter.

'Go on, then, mister,' I said, as he jumped down from the table. 'Bath and pyjamas on then, quickly, while we see to the feast.'

And half an hour later, looking every inch the normal happy family, the three of us were lined up on the sofa, munching popcorn while Dorothy and Toto had their adventures in the wonderful land of Oz. And not for the first time – and I doubted it would be the last time for that matter – I mused about how innocent and powerless children are in the scheme of their lives.

It was still a big ask, the whole thing with his mother, but, sitting there, I hoped with all my heart that there'd be something special at the end of Spencer's rainbow.

# Chapter 24

Tuesday morning began with two pieces of good news. The first took the form of a dawn answerphone message to let us know Spencer's school had finally reopened. For all that the Spencer we had right now was the variety we liked (rather than the naughty one) he needed the routine of school back in his life – even more so with the emotional upheaval that, potentially, might be coming very soon.

And once I'd dropped him off and returned home – the snow having thawed enough, at last, to get the car out – the second piece of good news, when I called the letting agents, was that we could go and see the property I was so keen to visit, and that very lunchtime, as well. So I called Mike at work and made him do something unprecedented: take a lunch hour. And had him pick up the keys from the agency office on his way home.

And it was as if someone up there had decided they liked me, because when we drove to the house I fell in love with it immediately. The garden was even bigger than it had looked in the pictures, and though its branches were currently bare, and laden with dripping snow, I spotted something that felt like it was truly meant to be – what looked like a huge mature cherry tree. And, once inside, I could tell my first impressions had been the right ones. It was spacious and open plan and had a real family feel to it. It would need a bit of tarting up, and a full-on Casey clean-athon, in order to bring it up to my standards, but every-thing about it was so perfect for our needs that I felt amazed it hadn't occurred to us to make a move before. I even iden-tified, though the coming festivities had been so far from my mind, exactly where I could put my three Christmas trees.

'God,' said Mike. 'I get the heebie jeebies even *thinking* about Christmas. Can we keep it a bit more low key this year, do you think?'

'Certainly not,' I said, feeling a welcome surge of seasonal energy. 'Particularly this year with Spencer – because, let's face it, there's still a good chance he'll still be with us, isn't there? No, we've got to make it magical. Unforgettable. The best Christmas ever …'

Mike raised his hand and shook his head. 'Love, I don't know why I even asked that.'

And the following day brought even better news for Spencer, though, to be truthful, it also filled me with anxi-ety. Once Spencer knew the facts – well, whatever portion of them Glenn felt was appropriate at this stage – it was going to be like letting the genie out of the bottle. Once Spencer knew the truth about his family, there would be no unknowing it, and though, as a child, with support, he would adapt to the new circumstances, it would still be incredibly emotionally destabilising for him to have to mentally re-write the memories of his whole life.

But when John phoned to update me on progress with Kerry, he seemed altogether less fearful than I was.

'She's definitely pressing charges against her husband,' he told me. 'I've met the sister now, and I think she's been a major force for good. I'm not sure she'd have had the wherewithal without her support, but right now it's all looking 100 per cent positive.'

'That's so good to know,' I said. 'As long as it lasts, that's the big thing.'

'Well, all we can do is hope it does,' he said pragmatically. 'But she's certainly beginning to get a solid base in place. She's obviously got her social worker – Christina, a lovely woman – and they seem to get on brilliantly. And they've also now assigned her a support worker as well.'

This was good. A support worker was a key – well – support. They wouldn't necessarily have a degree, or the same level of training as a social worker, but they usually had experience of working with children and their families, and were very much the people who worked at the coal face, helping parents in difficulty with establishing boundaries as well as assisting with day-to-day tasks that some parents found daunting, such as getting kids to dental appointments, form filling, getting access to benefits and so on. Kerry, I had no doubt, would need help with such matters, now she was going it alone for the first time.

'And with that kind of help she has every chance of coping,' John went on. 'And both Christina and her support worker seem confident she has the strength to kick the drink into touch. I know it's a big ask – we're neither of us that naïve, are we, Casey, eh? – but when diehard gloom merchants like support workers and social workers start bandying words like "positive" and "confident" around you know you're in with a fighting chance.'

I laughed. John had a point: people who worked in social services – not to mention people like me and Mike – routinely saw so many bad things in their line of work that if they felt positive about something or someone it really counted for something. 'That's really reassuring,' I agreed. 'So what's the next step, then?'

'Well, Christina is obviously working around the clock to get her and the kids housed so that she can leave the refuge, and everyone's hopeful that can happen before Christmas. But the key thing is that she feels Kerry's made sufficient progress that the time is right to arrange a meeting with young Spencer. Somewhere local to you, though, so he feels comfortable and safe. Any suggestions? I was thinking a coffee place or something …'

'I know the perfect place,' I said. 'There's an ice-cream bar in town he loves going to. I bet he'd love the chance to go there with his mum.'

'What's the name?'

'Giorgio's. Just off the high street. D'you know it?'

'No, but I can find the address easily enough, I'm sure. So, how about after school on Friday? That's what Christina was thinking. She can head there with Kerry – about fourish? Give him time to get home and changed out of his uniform.'

'That'll be perfect,' I said, noting it down – though I really didn't need to. I felt quite sure this 'date' was going to dominate the remainder of my week. 'But how do I play it, John? Exactly how much do I tell him? As it happens, I have a letter he's written and wants to give her.' I explained about our correspondence session.

'Well, that's your opener, right there,' he said. 'Tell him we've arranged that they can meet so he can give it to her. Explain that his dad's not going to be there; that it'll just be the two of them – plus the social worker. I don't think you really need to say more than that. You could tell him his mum's missed him, of course, and that she was the one who asked to see him. Whatever happens after this, I don't think it'll hurt that kid one little bit to know that someone, besides you and Mike, of course, care that he's alive.'

I didn't either, and couldn't wait to tell Spencer the news. My little piece of it anyway; the real news, John explained, was for Kerry and Christina to tell him, once I'd dropped him at Georgio's come Friday. The first day, I thought, if somewhat melodramatically. The first day of the rest of Spencer's life.


'God,' Riley commented later on that day, after school, 'I don't know how you manage to keep it all in, Mum.'

She was round at ours, with the little ones, helping with some packing. Because, to our great relief, we'd heard we could definitely have the house and, since it was empty, and provided the paperwork was all signed, could also move in before Christmas. Literally *just* before Christmas – the 23rd, to be precise. We could have waited till January, but now the ball had started rolling, wild horses, however fleet of foot, couldn't have dragged me away. And it wasn't as if it would be as bad as all that. The removal men were booked – no problems there; they were understandably quiet at this time of year – so all we had to do was a little light streamlining really, just to stop us moving years of accumulated junk from one place to the next.

'Tell me about it,' I said. 'And of course it's doubly complicated, because Spencer obviously thinks he's moving with us. Which he well might be. Even if things go well, we don't yet know if moving back in with her is going to be viable. And even if he does, it might all go pear shaped again, mightn't it? In which case he'll be back again. Just have to see how it goes.'

This was normal practice, of course, in a situation such as this. While the new arrangement was being trialled, I'd not be offered another child. I needed to be ready to take Spencer back again, for however long was necessary, should going back to his mother not prove viable. It was something I didn't want to think about, for Spencer's sake mostly, but even if the worst happened I'd at least have a break in which to recharge my batteries and get us properly settled in. I kept my voice down when chatting to Riley about all this, as Spencer himself was only in the other room, entertaining Levi and Jackson; the three of them were busy sorting out the huge box of toys under the stairs, which I'd dragged out so they could sort what was in there into categories. 'So's we don't end up taking stuff I'm too old to play with,' he had told them. 'That can all go in a special box for when you two come round.'

'Which is all you can do,' Riley said now. 'That and cross your fingers. But you know what? Something tells me it will all work out fine. I don't know why – heaven help us; it's been one hell of a few months, hasn't it? – but I have a good feeling about this.'

'And there speaks Mystic Meg,' I laughed. 'Let's just hope you're right. And if it doesn't … well, I guess it'll just be sleeves up and crack on … though, right now, sleeves up and pack on is the priority. If we're ever to get it done before moving day, that is. And Christmas, for that matter. You know, I never thought I'd hear myself say this, but it's actually been rather good for me, I think, all this upheaval. I keep thinking about decorations and then remembering I can't do them. And finding it strangely relaxing. Most odd.'

Riley grinned. 'I never thought I'd hear you say that either,' she admitted. 'And speaking of which, I shall do Christmas again this year. No arguments, either. You've got enough on your plate.'

'But –'

'No buts, Mum. It's a done deal. And yes, I've already run it past David. And Kieron. We decided you can have a New Year's Eve party instead. Stroke housewarming party. Kieron'll be on his decks. It's all sorted. See if you can't start as you mean to go on, and fall out with your new neighbours as well as your old ones. Only kidding! A much more sensible idea, don't you think? See? I've thought of everything.'

'So have I,' came a voice from the doorway. It was Spencer. He was holding up his box of plastic dinosaurs which he now thrust towards Riley. 'We're done with the trunk, so I told the little ones they could play with my dinosaurs while I help you with whichever job is next. Is that all right, Riley? I wasn't sure if they were okay for Jackson. But there aren't any small parts, I don't think.' We both glanced at each other, thinking the same thing: how much this little boy should be back home with his own siblings.

By the time Friday afternoon came round I don't know which one of us was most sick with nerves – me or Spencer. 'I've had a funny electric feeling in my tummy all day,' he admitted once I'd got him home and had come upstairs to help him choose what to wear. He'd had it all sorted the evening before, but now he was dithering, just a symptom, I knew, of his extreme anxiety about seeing his mother.

He wasn't stupid: he had taken in what I'd told him calmly enough – that it was a contact visit with Mum only, so that he could give her his letter – but he knew there was an emotional tension to this meeting, even if he couldn't consciously articulate it. In the end he plumped for jeans, but discarded a favourite hoodie for the shirt I had bought him the previous weekend, ironically to replace one he'd ripped when he trashed his room. We'd chosen it together, from a catalogue, and I was touched. He clearly wanted to feel just that little bit more formal, and, maybe, I thought, allowing myself just a hint of sentimentality, to have a bit of me on side, as a kind of security blanket.

Mike was coming too, and had come home from work early. He wanted to be there not just because there'd be two of us to provide solidity and reassurance, but also because while Spencer met with his mother I'd have to hang around in town, and on pins. There was also the matter of Spencer's father in all this. We didn't know precisely how much his mother was going to tell him, but one thing he probably did need to know at this stage was that the person he knew as Dad wasn't going to be in his life for the foreseeable future, which knowledge, even if they didn't yet spell out his real parentage, was a lot for any child to take in.

'Do I look all right?' he said, the clothes finally on, his expression anxious. I was standing ready, brandishing the hairbrush. I beckoned him over. 'You look perfect, Spencer Herrington,' I told him seriously, as he was subjected to a thorough brushing of his unruly locks. It wasn't the sort of thing most eight-year-old boys would willingly subject themselves to, but then Spencer wasn't like most eight-year-old boys and this wasn't the sort of situation most eight-year-old boys would find themselves in; meeting their mother, who'd abandoned them, and with just the one wish – that she love them again. Such a little and yet such a lot to ask. I felt as tense as an over-wound grandfather clock. *The boy in care at number 57.* The phrase haunted me. I so hoped he wouldn't have to be that any more. And not just because Mike and I were changing our address.

'There,' I said, finally. 'You'll do. Come on, sweetheart. Let's be off.'

'You coming in as well?' he asked as we headed down the stairs to where Mike waited.

I shook my head. 'I can't, sorry. I'm on my pre-Christmas diet. Tell you what; you have an extra ice cream for me.'

However, by the time we got to Giorgio's it occurred to me that ice cream would be the very last thing on Spencer's mind. Given that my own response to seeing her felt almost physical – a real jolt – I couldn't imagine quite how on edge her son must be. She was sitting at the window, with another woman – which would be Christina – at a table I imagined they had chosen for the purpose. She spotted Spencer and waved a hand in greeting, and his hand gripped mine tightly, while the other furiously brushed away tears.

I slackened my own grip. 'Go on, then,' I whispered, 'off you go. Christina'll ring us when you're done, okay? Good luck.'

'I can't tell you quite how much I need a coffee and a fag right now,' I told Mike as we watched them. They'd dissolved into each other's arms now and we could see from their body language that both, looked on by a smiling Christina, were in floods of uncontrollable tears. Not that tears ever solved the world's ills, not alone. It would take a lot more. I felt suddenly clear-headed, even without the fag. What would be would be.

Mike placed his arm around my shoulder. 'Coffee, definitely,' he agreed. We took ourselves off to our own favourite coffee emporium, further down the street. We'd wait there till Christina called us. A first. The carols were being piped and the tinsel hung gaily, but Christmas shopping could wait a bit longer.

'Wouldn't it be brilliant,' I said to Mike, as I wrapped both hands around my coffee mug. 'Wouldn't it just be so incredibly brilliant if, just for once, things turned out in a way that the system, for *all* its experience, still liked to believe are possible? Even though, mostly, they don't? Wouldn't it be wonderful if the impossible could happen, don't you think? That a child who's in care – a child who's come to *us*, moreover – could be reunited with his family?'

Mike sipped his own coffee and nodded as he did so. 'Fingers crossed,' he said.

We both crossed them.

# Chapter 25

'Guess what, Casey? Oh, you'll never guess! Oh my God! Just come get me. I've got big, big news!'

Mike and I had been so immersed in our discussions that when my mobile vibrated into life on the table between us we both almost jumped out of our seats.

We both smiled at Spencer's choice of expression, as well. How lovely, we agreed, as we trotted back down the high street and round the corner to Giorgio's, that the kids we fostered would adopt so many of our family expressions. It felt like a good omen. We couldn't wait to hear what 'big, big news' he had for us.

The windows of the ice-cream parlour were foggy with condensation, but even through the blur we couldn't fail to spot the smiles on everyone's faces. And when he saw us, Spencer looked like he was about to go off pop.

Kerry's expression was more muted once she made eye contact with the pair of us, but that didn't surprise me. She must have found it incredibly hard to face us, and I understood. We greeted her warmly, and while I slipped into the fourth spare seat at the table Christina stood up, pleading a need for the ladies, and allowing Mike to slip into her seat while Spencer told us his news.

He looked at his mum first, still beaming, and saying, 'Mum, I think I should tell them. I think you've had enough excitement for one day.'

This proved to be the perfect ice-breaker, because it had all of us in stitches, even though Spencer couldn't understand why we were laughing so hard.

Looking at Kerry more closely, I was stunned by the transformation. I could tell she'd been crying – the evidence was both in her eyes and in the big ball of tissue clutched in her hand – but apart from that, it was like looking at a different woman. Though it was probably hard to see unless the life transformation was as dramatic as hers had been, it really struck me just how toxic a poison alcohol could be. I enjoyed a drink myself, but it certainly brought it home to me: this woman's face had gone from ravaged grey shell to rounded human countenance. Yes, she had a way to go, clearly, and yes, she still had the evidence of all she'd been through in her features, but the twinkle of happiness in her eyes, and the fact that she looked at least ten years younger than the last time I had seen her, were good enough for me. Good enough for me to believe that she could get there.

'Hark at you,' she said now. 'Sound like a proper little grown-up.'

'Go on, then,' I chipped in. 'What's this big, big news, then?'

Spencer babbled excitedly for a good five minutes. About how he'd told his mum about how we'd fixed him, and how she'd really loved her letter (that ball of tissues, I thought to myself, might have come into its own at that point) and how she was going to live in a new place – 'Just like you an' Mike. Isn't that funny?' – because his dad had to go away for a bit, and she needed to be near his auntie, and how he couldn't wait to meet her as well, and that the best bit of all was that she wanted him to come home again, and that now he was being fixed they were going to arrange so he could go for a sleepover. 'An' a long one, as well. Not just for the night or the weekend. It's going to be like for a trial,' Spencer explained as Christina returned to the table and perched on an adjacent one while we wrapped everything up. 'Just so's we can make sure that everything's okay, and that.'

'That's fantastic, mate,' said Mike. 'Really pleased for you. We both are.' He turned to Christina. 'So when are we talking about this happening?'

'I just have to run things by Glenn,' she explained, having ordered a fresh round of drinks for us all. 'But if he has no objections, I see no reason why we can't organise this as soon as Kerry's settled into her new home. She's been allocated a place now, which we're off to look at after this, actually.' She smiled at Kerry. 'Which certainly seems to fit the bill on paper, so, well, let's keep everything crossed it does.'

'And I told Mum, I'm really good at packing and unpacking stuff, aren't I, Casey?' Spencer beamed. 'So I can help her make it nice, an' that, can't I?' His smile really lit the room up, which was so wonderful to see. If bittersweet. 'So it's not all wrecked,' he finished.

My heart remained firmly in my mouth for the next few days, even so. What sounded like such a straightforward business from a booth in an ice-cream parlour on a twinkly December afternoon was in reality anything but. Spencer wasn't a ward of court, but he was in the care of social services, and social services, quite rightly, did not just plonk children in their care back into family situations that felt anything less than tenable. It would not only be deeply irresponsible and potentially dangerous, it would also go against everything they stood for in their role as state guardians, by giving the child an even greater number of issues than they first came with.

That said, superficially this all looked workable. Glenn called us himself that evening, and we arranged for him to come and see Spencer because it was obviously important that this step was one he really wanted, as opposed to one he was going along with because he was anxious to please. This wasn't as unlikely a potential scenario as it might have sounded. However much Spencer craved the love of his mother, it might have been that he felt more comfortable, at least in the short term, staying with me and Mike and doing regular contact visits with his mother. Had that been his preference then that would have been what would have happened.

But it wasn't. Spencer's need for his mother felt almost physical; as well it might, since he had craved her love and care all his life. I couldn't help but hope – even if it was simplistic – that it would be the magic ingredient that would set him straight. Because a mother's love, after all, was the most natural thing in the world.

Penny also joined us that evening to chat to Spencer about continuing with his counselling because, as she told him, Rome wasn't built in a day.

'What's Rome got to do with it?' he wanted to know. 'Where's Rome anyway?'

He had Fluffy Cow fixed on his hand – something I'd not seen in a while now.

'It's in Italy,' she told him. 'Where the Romans used to live. You've heard of Romans?'

Spencer nodded. 'I think so.'

'Well, they built lots of fine buildings. But it took a long time, as you'd expect …'

'More than a day,' Spencer interrupted.

'Exactly,' said Penny, grinning. 'And it's the same with you, Spencer.'

'But I thought Casey and Mike had fixed me.' He looked at me. 'I thought I was fixed now, so that's why I can go home again.'

Penny reached across and gently squeezed one of his biceps. Then she waggled his arm. 'Hmm, yup. Well, yes, I must admit, you do seem pretty fixed. All working perfectly, as far as I can see. But that's not the whole story.' Her expression grew serious. 'You still need to understand where all that anger inside you came from …' Spencer looked perplexed. 'The anger that you might not have seen as anger, but that made you do some of the things you've been doing. Some of the things that you know are bad, and that have got you into trouble with the police. That's what I mean. That's what we still need to deal with. Where it's come from and how to deal with it whenever it comes back, okay?' Spencer nodded. 'Will it then, d'you think?'

'Not too much, I hope. But, yes, maybe. Because ...' Spencer grinned. 'Rome wasn't built in a day.'

Not that Spencer wasn't just a little bit peeved at this development. He'd been impeccably behaved both during his chat with Glenn and his one with Penny, but he still had his own ideas about how things should go now. 'She should butt out, that social worker,' he observed tetchily once the house was again quiet and he was preparing for bed. 'Now I'm going back home and I'm all fixed an' that. I'm *fine*.'

'Yes, you probably are, love,' I said, sitting down on the bed. 'But you must remember, social services are there to help you. To make things better. And not just you, remember, your mum too. Remember what I said to you about sometimes it's the grown-ups that need the most fixing?' He nodded. 'Well, this is as much about your mum as it is about you.'

'And what about my dad?' he asked. He wasn't looking at me, and I had a hunch that was intentional.

'I don't know, love,' I said levelly. 'I don't really know your dad, do I? What do you think?'

'I think I like it just with my mum,' he said. 'And Lewis an' that ... And the others. For now.'

The edge in his voice was obvious. 'Don't worry. I think Glenn knows that,' I said to him. 'Don't you?'

\* \* \*

I don't think I can remember another run-up to Christmas that was anything like it. Which is understandable, perhaps. It's not every day you move home only days before the holidays and at the same time prepare for what will hopefully be the permanent departure for a foster child who has dominated your lives for five months. Not that hoping for permanence in this case was anything but the right thing. We'd miss Spencer: for all the stress and trauma we'd been through, he'd got under our skins as surely as any other child could, perhaps more so because we'd believed such bad things about him, on the basis of what had turned out to be so far from the truth. And also, perhaps, because it was in Mike's and my DNA. Certainly, as we packed up and cleared out and cleaned, our principal feeling was that without a child running around it, home, for us, didn't feel homely.

But it would soon be the case, and I knew I should feel grateful. An overnight visit to his mum's new home, shortly after she and his half-siblings moved in, had gone brilliantly. We knew nothing of the detail, but then again we didn't need to. Glenn's report back, together with Spencer's excitement, told us all we needed to know on that score.

And it was a boost I needed. It was particularly painful clearing out the last of Kieron's things – all his amps and his leads and his boxes and boxes of CDs, all of which were still carefully stowed in his bedroom, and would now have to find a home in his and Lauren's flat. And it wasn't just that it made no sense to move them to our new home, it was also a rite of passage – a tangible reminder that we had moved to the next stage. The last of our own children really had flown the nest.

But there was good news yet again, just a couple of days before he was due to leave us, when Spencer's youth-offending officer, after only his second visit, gave him a gratifyingly glowing report.

'You see, Casey, I am fixed!' he told me proudly, when I shared the gist of it with him. It was the day before Spencer was going – two days before our own move. It was beginning to make me feel quite un-Casey-like, all of it. I was having too much life to deal with, in one place, at one time. Our house now stood half-empty and we'd gradually been relocating boxes to the new one, and I constantly had the feeling that I might suddenly start to cry.

I was grateful school had finished, so that I had Spencer's physical presence in the house with me. And as he looked at me I realised he could see that too. He rushed over and gave me one of his knock-you-over bear hugs, scrunching the youth-offending officer's report between us.

'Don't you worry about me, Casey. I'll be fine now,' he told me. 'I'm gonna be nine soon and I can look after myself, honest!' In some ways, I thought, he never spoke a truer word.

'Thanks, babes,' I said. 'I really needed that cuddle. I know you'll be okay, but I'll miss you. We all will.'

Spencer thought for a minute, then pulled something out of his pocket. It was Fluffy Cow. 'Look,' he said, holding the little puppet out to me. 'How about you look after Fluffy Cow for a bit. So's you don't miss me so much.'

Casey Watson

I began to shake my head. 'I couldn't do that,' I said. 'Because he'd miss you too, then, wouldn't he? And I'd hate to think of both of us moping around. No, he's got to go with you, so you can chat about things together.'

He processed this. I could see him thinking it all through. 'I s'pose you're right,' he said, slipping the puppet over his hand. 'But I been thinking. If you ever need me to come over for a sleepover, just phone my mum, okay? She'll let me.'

After that, Spencer had no one but himself to blame when I scooped him up again and started showering him with kisses.

Mike came in then, another box in hand, bound for the car.

'Help!' said Spencer playfully, making Fluffy Cow's mouth move. My cue, I knew, to let him go. 'Phew,' he said. 'Mike, do you want me to come and help you? I have to get out of here before she starts all her kissing malarkey again!'

Malarkey. I sighed as I got back to my cleaning. Tomorrow he'd be gone, and though I knew we'd keep in touch this was never, I knew, going to get any easier.

'It's torture,' Mike agreed, 24 hours later, as Glenn's car, containing Spencer plus Fluffy Cow, plus the all-important dinosaurs, plus the Chipmunks CD we'd almost forgotten was still in *our* car, rounded the corner to take him to his new home and new life. 'But who would have thought it? I've spent whole weekends helping the police with their enquires, I've fallen out with almost every neighbour in the street, I've been threatened with violence, I've had holes

290

made in my walls, dents made in my car and half my tool-box has disappeared for ever …'

'Who'd have thought *what*?' I wanted to know, as we went back inside, and Mike crossed the room to close the living-room skylights. It was bitterly cold, but the snow had almost gone now. Instead it was a clear, sunny day. It shone on our empty rooms, looking for dust motes. It would be lucky.

Mike looked sheepish. 'Who would have thought that a nightmare kid like Spencer could get under your skin so flippin' much?'

'Tell me about it,' I agreed, blowing my nose hard, the noise echoing in our almost empty living room. The sofa sat between us sorrowfully, waiting to be re-homed, like we were. 'And this time, my love, I agree with you.'

'About what?'

'About something I've decided, that's all.' I circled the sofa and linked my arm through Mike's, still by the window. 'That this time we need a break before taking on the next one.'

'Did I hear you right?' he chuckled.

'Yes, astonishing though it may seem, yes you did.' I looked out, peering hopefully at the blue. We needed snow again. Snow and trees and fairy lights. Lots of fairy lights. I squeezed Mike's arm. 'Anyone up for Christmas?'

# Epilogue

We moved into our new home the day after Spencer left. It was just two days before Christmas and, in typical Watson style, the whole family rallied round. Within hours of moving in we had it festooned with fairy lights, garlands and a huge Christmas tree. Then we all went to Riley's and had a wonderful Christmas, together with our first foster child, Justin, as always. And, yes, we did have that New Year's Eve house-warming party, and made a point of inviting every one of our new neighbours. Money in the bank, so to speak.

Three years have passed, and Spencer is doing incredibly well. Now twelve, he attends the same comprehensive as his siblings and, always bright, is also doing well academically. He's also something of an accomplished artist now, as well, having had a painting chosen to be exhibited in the town hall as part of his school's art competition. He's also on the right track emotionally, we're told. Despite his reluctance, he attended counselling for a further six months after he left us, and has so far managed to keep himself out of trouble. His mother, Kerry, has kept her promise to Spencer, and still attends AA and is doing well. She also swims again, apparently, and both she and Spencer belong to a local swimming club.

The father, Danny, is just a memory for Spencer. Though he has supervised contact with Spencer's older siblings, he plays no part in either Spencer's or his younger siblings' lives.

As for my break, well, it turned out to be a short one. Though I did 'enjoy' the promised four weeks for settling into our new neighbourhood, John called, in early February, with details of a new child. A nine-year-old called Abigail had just come under the care of social services, having been sole carer for her mum, who had multiple sclerosis, and who was now much too ill to live at home any more.

A nine-year-old girl who'd been a carer? What could be simpler? I didn't even let him finish his sentence.

# CASEY WATSON

*One woman determined to make a difference.*

*Read Casey's poignant memoirs and be inspired.*

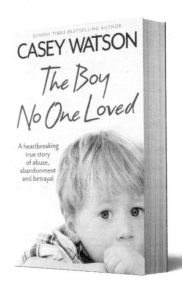

Five-year-old Justin was desperate and helpless

Six years after being taken into care, Justin has had 20 failed placements. Casey and her family are his last hope.

**THE BOY NO ONE LOVED**

A damaged girl haunted by her past

Sophia pushes Casey to the limits, threatening the safety of the whole family. Can Casey make a difference in time?

**CRYING FOR HELP**

Abused siblings who do not know what it means to be loved

With new found security and trust, Casey helps Ashton and Olivia to rebuild their lives.

## LITTLE PRISONERS

Branded 'vicious and evil' eight-year-old Spencer asks to be taken into care

Casey and her family are disgusted: kids aren't born evil. Despite the challenges Spencer brings, they are determined to help him find a loving home.

## TOO HURT TO STAY

# FEEL HEART.
# FEEL HOPE.
# READ CASEY.

Discover more about Casey Watson.
Visit www.caseywatson.co.uk

Find Casey Watson on  &